MORE THAN
SAMOOSAS

MORE THAN SAMOOSAS

EASY CAPE MALAY CUISINE WITH AN INDIAN TWIST

NAZEEHA ABRAHAMS

*I dedicate this book to
my mother, Abeeda Abrahams,
who has taught me everything
I know about cooking,
and who never fails to inspire me
with her new and innovative ideas!*

This book was published in Human
& Rousseau's fiftieth anniversary year.

First edition 2009
by Human & Rousseau
an imprint of NB Publishers
40 Heerengracht, Cape Town 8000

Copyright © published edition: Human & Rousseau (2009)
Copyright © text: Nazeeha Abrahams (2009)

No part of this book may be reproduced or transmitted in any form or by any electronic or mechanical means, including photocopying and recording, or by any other information storage or retrieval system, without written permission from the publisher.

Publisher: Tania de Kock
Editor and indexer: Joy Clack
Designer: PETALDESIGN
Photographer: Warren Heath
Stylist: Susan Bosman
Stylist's assistant: Justine Jacobs
Proofreader: Tessa Kennedy

Photography on pages 10, 26, 38, 50, 66, 86, 94, 102, 116, 126 and 142 by Jenna Zetisky.

Reproduction by Resolution Colour Pty (Ltd), Cape Town, RSA
Printed and bound by Tien Wah (Pte) Ltd, Singapore

ISBN-10   : 0-7981-4987-6
ISBN-13   : 978-0-7981-4987-7

Accessories supplied by courtesy of Milleu.

CONTENTS

INTRODUCTION	7
GLOSSARY OF INGREDIENTS	8
SOUPS AND ACCOMPANIMENTS	11
SEAFOOD AND FISH DISHES	27
CHICKEN AND POULTRY DISHES	39
MEAT DISHES	51
CURRIES AND BREYANIS	67
BREDIES AND STEWS	87
RICE	95
VEGETABLES AND SALADS	103
BREADS AND PASTRY	117
PUDDINGS, TARTS AND FRITTERS	127
CAKES AND BISCUITS	143
INDEX	160

INTRODUCTION

My passion for cooking started the day I became a wife. I had no choice but to learn quickly to prevent my husband from starving or from living on take-out every night.

I blame my mother for spoiling my two sisters and me, as we never helped much in the kitchen growing up. My mother loved cooking and never bothered asking for any help from us, which led to my dilemma the day I got married and realized that I would be responsible for feeding this man … my husband. I didn't know a thing about cooking, let alone preparing dishes suitable for human consumption!

Help was at hand. I spoke to my mother, who laughed at my problem and willingly offered to help. Every day I would spend a few hours with her, writing down recipes step by step as she explained them. I would then go home, prepare the food and amaze my husband every single night.

My cooking skills became so good that my husband soon started putting on weight and even mentioned that my cooking was way better than his mom's, which is the best compliment any wife can get from her husband!

Unlike myself, my mother started cooking Cape Malay dishes from the age of ten, acquiring her skills from her mother while living in Cape Town. She then moved to Durban with her family and lived there for many years before returning to the Cape. In Durban she learnt the Indian cooking style and was introduced to new, exotic spices. She combined what she had learnt with her own knowledge and therefore cooks like no other Cape Malay woman I know. 'It's all in the taste!' she always says, and that's the difference between these recipes and the traditional Cape Malay style of cooking.

I therefore would like to share my knowledge with everyone who is faced with the same problems I experienced or who just wants to learn how to cook. If I could do it then anyone can!

Nazeeha Abrahams
January 2009

GLOSSARY OF INGREDIENTS

ALLSPICE
These are small dried berries obtained from the pimento tree. They are used in bredies, curries, soups and certain desserts.

ANISEED
As the name suggests, it is the seed of the anise plant. It is used mainly in desserts and confectionery and has a similar flavour and fragrance to that of liquorice.

BARISHAP
Also known as fennel. It is used in ground form in breyanis and fish dishes.

BAY LEAVES
These leaves come from the laurel tree. They have a bitter taste and are used in meat dishes, soups, pickled fish and many bredies.

BREDIE
A type of stew, the flavour of which is based on the ingredients added to it. Onions and meat or chicken are braised together, with the vegetables being added thereafter.

BREYANI
This dish is made mainly of rice, but includes potatoes, eggs, spices, lentils, meat, chicken or fish depending on variant.

CARDAMOM
This spice is ground or used whole in a variety of dishes, including meat dishes, curries, soups, breyanis and desserts.

CHILLIES
Dried or fresh chillies can be used although one must remember that fresh chillies are hotter and should be used sparingly. Fresh chillies can be substituted with crushed chilli paste, which is readily obtainable at local food stores.

CINNAMON
Obtained from the bark of the cinnamon tree. It is used ground or in stick form to flavour various savoury and sweet dishes.

CLOVES
These are sun-dried, closed buds of clove trees and are used ground or whole in a variety of sweet and savoury dishes.

CURRY
This is a spiced, saucy dish with either meat, poultry or fish being the main ingredient. It is served with rice or roti.

CURRY LEAVES
Both dried and fresh curry leaves are available. The dried variation is used in curries, as this gives more flavour than fresh leaves.

CURRY POWDER
This is a combination of a variety of spices, including chilli powder, coriander, cumin, fenugreek, turmeric, cardamom and cloves. There are different variants such as mild, medium and strong.

DHAL
This is an Indian lentil used in curries and breyanis. It can be substituted with dried lentils found at your local food store.

DHANIA
Also known as coriander leaves, these are used fresh to add flavour to curries and other savoury dishes. Also available in powdered form and then known as ground coriander.

GARLIC
Used mainly in crushed form on its own or with added ginger paste. It is used in most savoury dishes.

GHEE
Also known as clarified butter, it can be bought ready-made from your local food store. It can be substitude by mixing one part cooking oil with two parts butter. Ghee can be kept indefinitely.

JEERA
Also known as cumin. Used mainly in curries and breyanis.

KHOKNI MASALA (WET)
This is a slightly moist combination of various spices. It is used in curries and breyanis. (This is an optional spice.)

LEAF MASALA
This is a combination of various spices and is used mainly in curries and breyanis.

METHI
Also known as fenugreek. Can be used ground or whole in various savoury dishes.

MOTHER-IN-LAW MASALA
This is a combination of various ground spices. It is used in curries and various savoury dishes. (This is an optional spice.)

MUSTARD SEEDS
These small black seeds are used to flavour savoury dishes.

POPADOMS
Popadoms can be obtained from most spice shops. They are fried in oil till crisp and are served as an accompaniment to many dishes.

PURI
This is a type of Indian bread that puffs up after being fried in oil.

ROTI
This is a type of Indian bread. It is flat, round and very flaky. Rotis are fried in ghee and served with curries or used to make salomies.

SAFFRON
This is an expensive spice obtained from the crocus flower. The stamens of the flower, which are orange in colour, are used to add flavour and colour to breyanis.

SMOOR
Another word for smoor would be braise, which means to fry lightly in oil or fat.

TURMERIC
This is a bright mustard spice used to colour and flavour many savoury dishes.

Note: The spices listed above as optional are not specifically required in the recipes contained in this book and can therefore be omitted.

SPICES TO KEEP IN YOUR CUPBOARD
Allspice (whole)
Aniseed (whole)
All-in-one masala
Barishap/Fennel (ground)
Bay leaves
Cardamom (whole)
Cayenne pepper
Chilli powder
Chilli flakes (dried)
Cinnamon (sticks and ground)
Cloves (whole)
Coriander (ground)
Curry powder/Red leaf masala (ground)
Curry leaves
Garam masala (ground)
Jeera/Cumin (ground)
Jeera seeds (whole)
Khokni masala (wet) (ground)
Methi masala/Fenugreek (ground)
Mother-in-law masala (ground)
Mustard seeds (whole)
Nutmeg (ground)
Peppercorns
Pepper (ground)
Seafood masala (ground)
Tandoori chicken masala (ground)
Turmeric (ground)

Soups are tasty, nourishing and economical meals to prepare; great for cold winter days or as a starter during the fasting month of Ramadan.

SOUPS AND ACCOMPANIMENTS

2.5 litres water

40 ml (8 tsp) chicken stock powder (optional)

5 carrots, scraped and sliced into rounds

2 large potatoes, peeled and cubed

3 leek stems, sliced into rounds

1 large onion, chopped

125 ml (½ cup) chopped celery

1 tomato, blanched, peeled and chopped

½ small butternut, peeled and cubed

8 whole peppercorns

10 ml (2 tsp) dried parsley

4 whole cloves

5 whole allspice

500 g chicken breast, cubed

10 ml (2 tsp) salt

5 ml (1 tsp) freshly ground black pepper

15 ml (1 Tbsp) sugar

5 ml (1 tsp) tomato paste

60 ml (¼ cup) cake flour

A great anytime meal or snack.

MAKES 2 LITRES

CHICKEN VEGETABLE SOUP

In a deep pot on medium heat, add 2 litres (8 cups) of the water and bring to the boil. Add the chicken stock powder, if using, and stir till dissolved.

In a blender or food processor, add half of the carrots, potatoes and leeks, plus all of the onion, celery, tomato and butternut. Add 250 ml (1 cup) of water and liquidize till it reaches a smooth consistency. Add this mixture to the pot of boiling stock, together with the peppercorns, parsley, cloves and allspice.

Add the remaining vegetables and the chicken, as well as the salt, pepper, sugar and tomato paste. Stir to combine. Simmer for 1 hour on medium heat. Mix the remaining 250 ml (1 cup) cold water with the cake flour till smooth and add to the soup. Stir to combine. Simmer for an additional 40 minutes, and then remove from the heat and serve with naan bread rolls or egg rolls.

Note: While the soup is cooking, remember to remove any foamy scum that rises to the surface, taking care not to discard any of the whole spices. All the soups in this chapter can be frozen for up to 3 weeks and reheated as required.

CREAMY CHICKEN AND CORN SOUP

MAKES ABOUT 2 LITRES

THIS IS A LIGHT, CREAMY SOUP, PERFECT TO SERVE AS A STARTER.

30 ml (2 Tbsp) butter or margarine
2 large onions, finely chopped
500 g chicken breast, cubed
10 ml (2 tsp) garlic and ginger paste
10 ml (2 tsp) salt
5 ml (1 tsp) freshly ground black pepper
5 ml (1 tsp) tandoori chicken spice
5 ml (1 tsp) mother-in-law masala
5 ml (1 tsp) methi masala
8 peppercorns
4 whole cloves
4 cardamom pods
2 pieces of stick cinnamon
2 litres (8 cups) boiling water
30 ml (2 Tbsp) chicken stock powder
1 x 410 g tin whole kernel corn, drained
1 x 420 g tin cream-style sweetcorn
250 ml (1 cup) cold water
60 ml (¼ cup) cake flour
500 ml (2 cups) fresh cream
125 ml (½ cup) chopped fresh dhania

In a deep pot on medium heat, melt the butter and braise the chopped onions lightly. Add the chicken cubes along with the garlic and ginger paste, salt, pepper, tandoori chicken spice, mother-in-law and methi masalas, peppercorns, cloves, cardamom and cinnamon. Braise.

In a separate bowl, mix the boiling water and chicken stock powder and add it to the pot. Add both tins of corn. Cook on medium heat for about 30 minutes.

Mix the cold water with the cake flour till smooth and add to the soup with the cream and dhania. Simmer for 20 minutes. Serve with naan bread.

Note: If preferred, 10 ml (2 tsp) white sugar can be added, or according to taste.

SPLIT PEA SOUP

MAKES ABOUT 2 LITRES

THIS IS A FILLING, NOURISHING SOUP TO SERVE AS A STARTER OR ON ITS OWN.

500 g stewing beef/soup meat
2 litres (8 cups) water
250 g dried split peas, boiled till soft
1 large onion
1 large potato
1 large turnip
3 carrots, scraped
2 tomatoes
125 ml (½ cup) chopped celery
250 ml (1 cup) frozen mixed vegetables
2 carrots, scraped and sliced into rounds
1 x 420 g tin cream-style sweetcorn
5 ml (1 tsp) dried parsley
6 peppercorns
6 whole allspice
6 whole cloves
5 ml (1 tsp) freshly ground black pepper
2.5 ml (½ tsp) garlic salt
2.5 ml (½ tsp) salt, or to taste
250 ml (1 cup) cold water
60 ml (¼ cup) cake flour

Wash and drain the meat. In a deep pot on medium heat, scorch the meat lightly and then add the 2 litres of water.

In a blender, liquidize the soft-boiled split peas till completely smooth. Add this to the water and meat in the pot. Liquidize the onion, potato, turnip, whole carrots, tomatoes and celery. Add this mixture to the pot along with the whole frozen veggies, carrot rounds, sweetcorn, dried parsley, peppercorns, allspice, cloves, black pepper, garlic salt and salt. Cook on medium heat for about 1 hour. Mix 250 ml (1 cup) cold water with the cake flour till smooth. Add to the soup, stir to combine and cook for a further 30 minutes. Serve with naan bread or kitke rolls.

375 ml (1½ cups) pea/chana flour or chilli bite mix
15 ml (1 Tbsp) cake flour
5 ml (1 tsp) baking powder
1 large onion, finely chopped or grated
1 large potato, coarsely grated
1 fresh green chilli, finely chopped
5 ml (1 tsp) salt
5 ml (1 tsp) turmeric
5 ml (1 tsp) ground jeera
2.5 ml (½ tsp) crushed dried chillies
2.5 ml (½ tsp) red leaf masala
5 ml (1 tsp) garlic and ginger paste
60 ml (¼ cup) chopped fresh dhania
About 125 ml (½ cup) cold water
About 500 ml (2 cups) cooking oil for deep-frying

A light anytime snack, or serve as an accompaniment to soup.

MAKES ABOUT 30

DHALTJIES (CHILLI BITES)

In a large mixing bowl, sift both flours and the baking powder. Add the remaining ingredients, except the water and oil, and mix with just enough of the water to form a stiff batter. Use more water if necessary, but note that the batter should be able to hold its shape and not be runny.

Heat the oil in a small, deep pot or pan on medium heat. Once the oil is hot, add a tablespoonful of batter, one spoon at a time, making sure not to overcrowd the pot and to allow space for turning the bites. Slowly fry on either side till golden brown and crisp. Monitor the temperature of the oil to ensure that it doesn't become too hot while frying.

Pierce the chilli bite with a fork to test if properly cooked: if the fork comes out dry, then the chilli bites are ready. Remove from the oil and drain in a colander or on paper towel.

Also known as potato warras, these make a great TV snack.

250 g (1¾ cup) chilli bite mix
125 ml (½ cup) cake flour
10 ml (2 tsp) baking powder
2.5 ml (½ tsp) salt, or to taste
2.5 ml (½ tsp) red leaf masala
2.5 ml (½ tsp) all-in-one masala
5 ml (1 tsp) turmeric
1 medium onion, finely chopped
2 fresh green chillies, finely chopped
6 lettuce leaves, shredded
2.5 ml (½ tsp) garlic and ginger paste
60 ml (¼ cup) chopped fresh dhania
2 large potatoes, cubed and steamed
250 ml (1 cup) cold water
500 ml (2 cups) cooking oil for deep-frying

MAKES ABOUT 30

POTATO BITES

In a large bowl, sift all of the dry ingredients. Add the onion, chillies, shredded lettuce, garlic and ginger paste and dhania. Fold the steamed potato cubes (they shouldn't be too soft) carefully into the mixture. Lastly, add the cold water and mix carefully, ensuring that all the ingredients are combined and form a thick batter that holds its shape easily. If the batter is not thick enough, add more flour.

Heat the oil in a small, deep pot or pan on medium heat. Once the oil is hot, reduce heat slightly. Place tablespoonsful of the mixture into the oil, one at a time, and fry slowly till golden brown on all sides and crisp. Pierce the warras with a fork to test if properly cooked. If the fork comes out dry, they are cooked. Remove from the oil and drain in a colander or on paper towel.

This is a nourishing broth similar to a soup, but it is slightly thicker and more filling.

5 ml (1 tsp) jeera seeds
2 fresh green chillies, finely chopped
1 large onion, finely chopped
60 ml (¼ cup) oil
750 g chicken breast, cubed or
500 g soup meat
5 ml (1 tsp) ground jeera
5 ml (1 tsp) salt
2.5 ml (½ tsp) turmeric
2.5 ml (½ tsp) dried chilli flakes
5 ml (1 tsp) freshly ground black pepper
4 cardamom pods
4 whole cloves
2 pieces of stick cinnamon
10 ml (2 tsp) garlic and ginger paste
2.5 litres water
375 g ready-made haleem mix
30 ml (2 Tbsp) ghee
5 ml (1 tsp) garam masala
60 ml (¼ cup) chopped fresh dhania

SERVES ABOUT 6

HALEEM

In a soup pot on medium heat, braise the jeera seeds, green chillies and onion in the oil till lightly golden. Add the washed meat along with the spices – excluding the garam masala – and the garlic and ginger paste, and braise till the meat is well coated. Add the water and cook on medium heat till the meat is tender.

Add the haleem mix to the pot and cook for a further 2 hours till the haleem has the consistency of broth. Lastly, add the ghee, garam masala and chopped dhania and simmer on low heat for 15 minutes. Remove from heat and serve with naan bread.

Note: The ready-made haleem mix can be purchased from most food stores and supermarkets specialising in halaal foods.

SAMOOSAS

SAMOOSA PUR (STRIPS) MAKES 48

DOUGH
375 ml (1½ cups) cold water
5 ml (1 tsp) lemon juice
750 ml (3 cups) cake flour
5 ml (1 tsp) salt

THESE TRIANGULAR-SHAPED PASTRIES WITH VARIOUS FILLINGS ARE OF INDIAN ORIGIN. THEY MAKE A DELICIOUS ANYTIME SNACK AND ARE GREAT TO SERVE ON THEIR OWN WITH A DIP OR AS AN ACCOMPANIMENT TO SOUPS.

Preheat the oven to 100 °C.

Mix the water and lemon juice in a jug and set aside. Sift the flour and salt into a large mixing bowl. Add the water to the flour mixture and combine to make a fairly stiff dough. Divide the dough into 12 equal portions and roll each portion between your palms into smooth, egg-sized balls.

Work with six portions at a time: On a floured surface, roll out the six balls as thinly as possible, into 6–8 cm diameter discs. Pile the discs on top of each other, smearing each with melted ghee and sprinkling each disc with a little flour. Leave the underside of the bottom disc and the top side of the top disc ungreased and unfloured. Roll out the pile of discs into one large disc, about 12 cm in diameter. Trim the sides to form a large square. Place the large pastry square on an ungreased baking sheet and bake in the oven for 2–3 minutes, or as soon as the layers show signs of loosening. Be careful not to burn the pastry while baking.

When slightly cooled, trim and cut the pur into 5-cm-wide and 25-cm-long strips. Separate the layers and stack them on top of each other. Wrap in a damp cloth to prevent the pur from drying out. Set aside for filling.

Holding a strip of pur in one hand, pull the top left-hand corner across to the right, with the edge slightly overlapping the right-hand side of the strip. Now fold this folded section over to the left, so that the top side now touches the left side, forming a triangular pocket. Turn the strip so that the point of the triangle faces you. Hold the triangular pocket gently and fill with the filling of your choice. Once filled, fold down the strip to cover the filling. Continue folding in the same fashion, keeping the triangular shape, till the entire strip is used, leaving a small flap that should be pasted down onto the samoosa with paste.

To make the paste, mix 125 ml (½ cup) cake flour with a little cold water till smooth. Seal the ends of the samoosa as well to prevent the filling from escaping during frying.

Over medium heat, deep-fry in hot oil till golden brown. Remove from the pot and drain on paper towel.

SAMOOSA FILLINGS
MINCE FILLING

FILLS 48 SAMOOSAS

60 ml (¼ cup) cooking oil
2 large onions, finely chopped
6 peppercorns
5 ml (1 tsp) jeera seeds
1 kg steak mince, washed and drained
10 ml (2 tsp) red leaf masala
10 ml (2 tsp) mother-in-law masala
5 ml (1 tsp) all-in-one masala
5 ml (1 tsp) turmeric
5 ml (1 tsp) ground jeera
2.5 ml (½ tsp) chilli powder
2.5 ml (½ tsp) salt, or to taste
4 fresh green chillies, finely chopped
15 ml (1 Tbsp) garlic and ginger paste
1 large onion, coarsely chopped
125 ml (½ cup) chopped fresh dhania

Heat the oil in a medium-sized pot on medium heat. Add the 2 finely chopped onions to the oil along with the peppercorns and jeera seeds and braise till golden brown. Add the mince to the onion mixture and stir thoroughly to combine. Add the spices, salt, chillies and garlic and ginger paste and mix thoroughly. Reduce heat slightly and simmer for 20 minutes. Lastly, add the remaining onion and the dhania and mix to combine. Simmer for an additional 5 minutes, then remove from heat and allow to cool. Transfer to a bowl and set aside for filling samoosas.

Note: The filling must be semi-dry as this prevents it from seeping out through the ends of the samoosa.

VEGETABLE FILLING

FILLS 48 SAMOOSAS

To a medium-sized pot on medium heat, add the cooking oil, jeera seeds and mustard seeds. When the oil is hot, add the chopped onions and braise till golden brown. Add the cold water and then immediately add the frozen vegetables. Simmer for about 10 minutes. Add the green chillies, garlic and ginger paste, salt and all the spices to the veggie mixture in the pot and stir thoroughly. Reduce heat and simmer for a further 10 minutes, or till the veggies are cooked. Add dhania and cook for a further 5 minutes, or till all of the water has cooked away. Remove from heat and transfer to a bowl. Allow to cool completely before filling the samoosas.

45 ml (3 Tbsp) cooking oil
5 ml (1 tsp) jeera seeds
2.5 ml (½ tsp) black mustard seeds
2 large onions, finely chopped
60 ml (¼ cup) cold water
1 kg frozen chopped mixed vegetables (peas, carrots and corn)
2 fresh green chillies, finely chopped
10 ml (2 tsp) garlic and ginger paste
2.5 ml (½ tsp) salt, or to taste
6 peppercorns
5 ml (1 tsp) turmeric
5 ml (1 tsp) chilli powder
5 ml (1 tsp) wet khokni masala
10 ml (2 tsp) mother-in-law masala
10 ml (2 tsp) red leaf masala
125 ml (½ cup) chopped fresh dhania

CHEESE FILLING

FILLS ABOUT 48 SAMOOSAS

In a large bowl, mix all of the ingredients together thoroughly. Cover the bowl and place in the refrigerator for 15 minutes before using the mixture to fill the samoosas.

750 ml (3 cups) coarsely grated Cheddar or sweetmilk (Gouda) cheese
1 x 340 g tin whole kernel corn, drained
1½ large onions, finely chopped
4 fresh green chillies, finely chopped
1 ml (¼ tsp) garlic and ginger paste
2.5 ml (½ tsp) chilli powder
60 ml (¼ cup) chopped fresh dhania
Salt to taste

CHICKEN FILLING

FILLS ABOUT 48 SAMOOSAS

60 ml (¼ cup) cooking oil
2 large onions, finely chopped
6 peppercorns
5 ml (1 tsp) jeera seeds
1 small green pepper, finely chopped
1 kg chicken mince, washed and drained
7.5 ml (1½ tsp) red leaf masala
5 ml (1 tsp) tandoori chicken masala
5 ml (1 tsp) all-in-one masala
10 ml (2 tsp) mother-in-law masala
5 ml (1 tsp) ground jeera
5 ml (1 tsp) turmeric
2.5 ml (½ tsp) chilli powder
2.5 ml (½ tsp) salt, or to taste
3 fresh green chillies, finely chopped
15 ml (1 Tbsp) garlic and ginger paste
1 x 340 g tin whole kernel corn, drained
1 large onion, coarsely chopped
125 ml (½ cup) chopped fresh dhania

To a medium-sized pot on medium heat, add the cooking oil and heat up. When the oil is hot, add the 2 finely chopped onions along with the peppercorns and jeera seeds, and braise for 3 minutes. Add the green pepper and braise till the onions are golden brown in colour. Add the chicken mince to the onion mixture in the pot and stir thoroughly to combine. Add the spices, salt, chillies and garlic and ginger paste and stir through. Add the corn and stir to combine and then simmer for about 20 minutes. Lastly, add the coarsely chopped onion and the dhania. Stir through, reduce heat slightly and simmer for an additional 5 minutes. Remove from heat and transfer to a large bowl. Allow to cool completely before filling samoosas.

SOUPS AND ACCOMPANIMENTS

Fish has always been popular with both Malays and Indians, as many caught fish as a means of earning their livelihood, or to feed their families.

SEAFOOD AND FISH DISHES

FISH FRIKKADELS

MAKES ABOUT 16

THIS MAKES A DELICIOUS LIGHT MEAL, SERVED WITH WHITE RICE OR MASH, AND TOMATO SMOOR.

2 x 125 g tins chunky tuna
1 large egg
1 fresh green chilli, finely chopped
1 medium onion, finely chopped
10 ml (2 tsp) dried parsley
60 ml (¼ cup) finely chopped celery
2.5 ml (½ tsp) garlic and ginger paste
1 ml (¼ tsp) freshly ground black pepper
1 ml (¼ tsp) ground jeera
2.5 ml (½ tsp) turmeric
1 ml (¼ tsp) fish masala
4 slices stale white bread
5 ml (1 tsp) salt, or to taste
60 ml (¼ cup) finely chopped fresh dhania
250 ml (1 cup) cooking oil

Drain the tuna in a colander and then transfer to a large mixing bowl. Add the egg, chilli, onion, parsley, celery, garlic and ginger paste, and all of the spices, except the salt. Place the bread in cold water for about 2 minutes till soaked. Squeeze out the excess water from the bread and add the bread to the tuna mixture. Lastly, add the salt and dhania. Mix thoroughly till all of the ingredients are combined.

Take a tablespoonful of mixture and roll it into a ball between your palms. Slightly flatten the top and bottom of the ball, forming a thick patty. Repeat with the rest of the tuna mixture. Heat a pan with shallow oil on medium heat and slowly fry the frikkadels for about 4 minutes on each side, or till brown in colour. Remove from the pan and drain on paper towel. Serve as mentioned above.

SALMON SMOOR

SERVES 6

A LIGHT SNACK SERVED ON TOASTED ROLLS OR BREAD. THE SALMON CAN ALSO BE SUBSTITUTED WITH TUNA IF DESIRED.

2 x 125 g tins salmon or chunky tuna
45 ml (3 Tbsp) cooking oil
1 large or 2 medium onions, finely chopped
2.5 ml (½ tsp) jeera seeds
6 peppercorns
30 ml (2 Tbsp) water
2 tomatoes, halved and finely grated
5 ml (1 tsp) garlic and ginger paste
1 whole green chilli, slit midway
30 ml (2 Tbsp) Worcestershire sauce
5 ml (1 tsp) salt
2.5 ml (½ tsp) red leaf masala
2.5 ml (½ tsp) chilli powder
A good pinch of chopped fresh dhania

Drain the salmon or tuna and set aside.

To a shallow pot on medium heat, add the cooking oil and heat up. Add the onion, jeera seeds and peppercorns and braise till golden brown in colour. Add the water along with the grated tomatoes, garlic and ginger paste, whole chilli, Worcestershire sauce, salt and spices, and simmer for 10 minutes.

Add the drained salmon and dhania and simmer for an additional 5 minutes. Remove from heat and allow to cool completely before serving as described above.

1 medium fresh snoek
10 ml (2 tsp) salt, or to taste
1–2 fresh green chillies
A good pinch of chopped fresh dhania
7.5 ml (1½ tsp) garlic and ginger paste
5 ml (1 tsp) ground jeera
2 x 60 ml (¼ cup) cooking oil
125 g butter or margarine, melted
5 ml (1 tsp) fish masala
5 ml (1 tsp) red leaf masala
5 ml (1 tsp) wet khokni masala
2.5 ml (½ tsp) turmeric
1 ml (¼ tsp) chilli powder
125 g butter or margarine, cubed
1 large tomato, thickly sliced
1 large green pepper, thickly sliced into rings
1 large onion, thickly sliced

SERVES 6–8

Any other fresh fish, such as kingklip, hake or yellowtail, can be used for this recipe, depending on preference.

BAKED SNOEK

Preheat the oven to 180 °C.

Remove the head and tail from the fish and scrape off most of the scales. Slit the fish open midway and wash thoroughly. After cleaning the fish, pat dry with paper towel. Place the opened fish in a large enough roasting pan and rub all over with salt.

In a blender, liquidize the green chillies, dhania, garlic and ginger paste and jeera powder with 60 ml (¼ cup) cooking oil till well infused. Mix the melted butter with the remaining cooking oil and to this add all the spices and mix well. Add the dhania-chilli mixture to the spice mixture and mix thoroughly. This will be used to marinate the fish.

Rub the marinade all over the fish till well coated. Cover and leave to stand for 15 minutes to allow the flavours to infuse. Place cubes of butter all over the fish, along with a few slices of tomato and green pepper, and the onion rings. Place in the oven and bake for 20–25 minutes, or till cooked. Place directly under the oven grill for an additional 5 minutes. Remove from the oven and serve with fried potato wedges, salads and rolls.

FISH CAKES

MAKES ABOUT 12

ANY FROZEN FISH FILLETS CAN BE USED FOR THIS RECIPE, DEPENDING ON PREFERENCE. IT MAKES A DELICIOUS LIGHT MEAL SERVED WITH BRAISED WHITE RICE AND TOMATO GRAVY OR POTATO WEDGES AND DIP.

500 g (5 steaklets) frozen hake or any fish of choice
5 ml (1 tsp) salt
5 ml (1 tsp) dried crushed chillies
2.5 ml (½ tsp) garlic and ginger paste
2.5 ml (½ tsp) grated nutmeg
2.5 ml (½ tsp) fish masala
2.5 ml (½ tsp) Cajun spice
1 large potato, cooked and mashed
60 ml (¼ cup) chopped fresh dhania
30 ml (2 Tbsp) butter or margarine
1 large egg, beaten
Breadcrumbs for coating
Cooking oil for frying

Poach the fish in a little water, on medium heat, till the water has cooked away and the fish becomes white in colour. Allow to cool slightly.

Transfer to a mixing bowl, flake the fish and remove all the bones (if any). Add the remaining ingredients, except the egg and breadcrumbs, and mix well. Take heaped dessertspoons of mixture and shape into 1-cm-thick, round fish cakes. Dip into the beaten egg, and then into the breadcrumbs to coat entire cake. Refrigerate for 10 minutes before frying.

Fry in a pan of shallow oil, on a medium to high heat, till golden brown on both sides. Drain on paper towel and serve warm as described above.

GREEN MASALA KINGKLIP

ANY FRESH LINE FISH MAY BE USED FOR THIS RECIPE.

SERVES 6

1 medium fresh fish, scaled and gutted
5 ml (1 tsp) ground jeera
2.5 ml (½ tsp) freshly ground black pepper
5 ml (1 tsp) crushed fresh green chillies
7.5 ml (1½ tsp) crushed garlic
125 ml (½ cup) finely chopped fresh dhania
15 ml (1 Tbsp) lemon juice
30 ml (2 Tbsp) cooking or olive oil
5 ml (1 tsp) salt
1 small green or red pepper, sliced into rings

Preheat the oven to 180 °C. Firstly, remove the head and tail of the fish. Wash the fish in cold water and blot off excess water with paper towel. Slit the fish midway, but not in half. Mix the jeera, black pepper, chillies, garlic, dhania, lemon juice and oil to form a paste. Rub the fish with the salt and then with the paste, coating the entire fish and using all of the paste.

Place the fish on a large piece of greased foil. Place a few green pepper rings inside the fish and on the top and wrap in the foil, forming a pocket by sealing the sides. Place the fish on a baking tray and bake in the preheated oven for about 45 minutes. Remove from the oven and serve with a noodle salad and fried potato wedges.

SEAFOOD AND FISH DISHES

This makes an exotic main meal served with savoury rice, stir-fried veggies and creamy garlic sauce.

1 kg fresh or frozen prawns
5 ml (1 tsp) salt, or to taste
2.5 ml (½ tsp) seafood or fish masala
2.5 ml (½ tsp) mother-in-law masala
2.5 ml (½ tsp) tandoori chicken spice
5 ml (1 tsp) Cajun spice
10 ml (2 tsp) lemon juice
10 ml (2 tsp) garlic and ginger paste
20 ml (4 tsp) crushed garlic
120 g butter or margarine

SERVES 6

GARLIC GRILLED PRAWNS

Wash the prawns in cold water, slit the shell down the centre, below the head of the prawn, and carefully remove the vein. Place the prawns in a large mixing bowl and set aside. In a separate bowl, mix all of the remaining ingredients, except the butter, to form the marinade. Add the marinade to the prawns, making sure the prawns are thickly coated with the spices. Cover and leave to stand in the refrigerator for 30 minutes before cooking. The prawns can either be grilled in the oven or prepared in a pot. Place the prawns in a large enough roasting pan. Melt the butter and pour it over the prawns – use more butter if required. Cover the roasting pan with foil and place under the preheated grill for 10–15 minutes. Remove the foil and grill for a further 5 minutes, or till the shells turn bright pink in colour. Serve as described above.

To prepare the prawns in a pot, place a deep pot on medium heat, add the butter and allow to heat up. Add the prawns to the pot and stir while cooking till the prawns turn pink in colour, about 8–10 minutes. Reduce the heat, cover with a lid and simmer for a further 5 minutes.

CREAMY GARLIC SAUCE

15 ml (1 Tbsp) butter or margarine
1 large onion, finely chopped
1 small green pepper, finely chopped
1 fresh green chilli, finely chopped
5 ml (1 tsp) freshly ground black pepper
2.5 ml (½ tsp) garlic salt
2.5 ml (½ tsp) mother-in-law masala
2.5 ml (½ tsp) dried parsley
2.5 ml (½ tsp) salt, or to taste
15 ml (1 Tbsp) crushed garlic
250 ml (1 cup) fresh cream
125 ml (½ cup) grated Cheddar cheese

In a saucepan on medium heat, add the butter and heat up. Add the onion, green pepper, chilli and black pepper. Braise till the onion is golden brown in colour. Add the garlic salt, masala, parsley, salt and garlic and stir well. Lastly, add the cream and grated cheese, and stir till the cheese has melted. Reduce heat and simmer for 5–8 minutes till slightly thickened. If you wish, a pinch of sugar can be added to slightly sweeten the sauce. Remove from heat and serve warm.

Note: This sauce makes a great accompaniment to any seafood dish.

SEAFOOD AND FISH DISHES

CAPE GRILLED CRAYFISH

SERVES 6

CRAYFISH IS AN ALL-TIME FAVOURITE TO SERVE ON EID DAY FOR LUNCH, EITHER GRILLED OR IN CURRY FORM.

6 whole crayfish
5 ml (1 tsp) mother-in-law masala
5 ml (1 tsp) seafood masala
5 ml (1 tsp) salt, or to taste
5 ml (1 tsp) tandoori chicken masala
10 ml (2 tsp) Cajun spice
5 ml (1 tsp) garlic salt
30 ml (2 Tbsp) crushed garlic
15 ml (1 Tbsp) lemon juice
60 ml (4 Tbsp) butter or margarine

Slit the crayfish through the middle, on the underside of the crayfish. Clean the chest cavity, but do not discard any of the meat. Carefully remove the vein from the tail and wash the crayfish under cold running water. Drain in a colander and blot dry with paper towel.

Mix all of the spices with the garlic and lemon juice to form a paste. Smear this paste all over the crayfish and on the inside. Place the crayfish, belly side down, in a large roasting pan. Melt the butter and pour it over the crayfish. Cover the roasting pan with foil and place directly under the oven grill for 15–20 minutes. Remove the foil, baste with melted butter mixed with a little garlic, and return to the oven to grill, uncovered, for a further 5–8 minutes. Remove from the oven and serve with savoury rice, stir-fried vegetables and creamy garlic sauce.

PICKLED FISH

SERVES 6

PICKLED FISH CAN BE SERVED AS A LIGHT MEAL WITH SALADS AND ROLLS. KINGKLIP, SNOEK, YELLOWTAIL OR KABELJOU CAN BE USED FOR THIS RECIPE.

1 medium fresh kingklip, in pieces
Salt and freshly ground black pepper to taste
250 ml (1 cup) cooking oil
4 large onions, sliced into rings
6 peppercorns
4 whole cloves
5 whole allspice
10 ml (2 tsp) garlic and ginger paste
10 ml (2 tsp) salt, or to taste
2 fresh green chillies
4 bay leaves
10 ml (2 tsp) fish masala
5 ml (1 tsp) turmeric
5 ml (1 tsp) chilli powder
250 ml (1 cup) water
375 ml (1½ cups) malt vinegar
125 ml (½ cup) sugar

Wash the fish, drain it in a colander and pat dry with paper towel. Sprinkle the fish with a little salt and black pepper. Heat a pan on medium heat and add 125 ml (½ cup) of cooking oil. Once the oil is hot enough, fry the fish till lightly golden brown in colour. Remove from heat and drain on paper towel. Place the fish in a large, shallow glass dish and set aside.

In a medium saucepan on medium heat, heat the remaining oil. Add the onions, peppercorns, cloves and allspice. Braise till the onions are golden brown in colour. Reduce heat and add the garlic and ginger paste, salt, chillies, bay leaves, fish masala, turmeric, chilli powder, water and simmer for 3 minutes. Add the vinegar and sugar and simmer for another 5–8 minutes on low heat. Remove from heat and allow onion mixture to cool slightly before pouring it over the fish. Make sure that all the fish is covered. Cover the dish with a lid and, only once completely cooled, store in the refrigerator for 24 hours before serving.

SEAFOOD AND FISH DISHES

This chapter covers quick and easy recipes for everyday cooking as well as meals for special occasions.

CHICKEN AND POULTRY DISHES

PEPPER CHICKEN POT ROAST

SERVES 8–10

THIS DISH IS VERY POPULAR WITH THE MALAY COMMUNITY AND MAKES A DELICIOUS SUNDAY LUNCH, SERVED WITH SWEET YELLOW RICE AND COMPLEMENTED BY A MEDLEY OF VEGETABLES.

12–20 chicken pieces, skinned (the skin may be left on if preferred)

10 ml (2 tsp) salt

15 ml (1 Tbsp) freshly ground black pepper

2.5 ml (½ tsp) chilli powder

5 ml (1 tsp) ground jeera

5 ml (1 tsp) garlic and ginger paste

60 ml (¼ cup) brown vinegar

45 ml (3 Tbsp) Worcestershire sauce

200 ml (¾ cup) water

5 medium potatoes, peeled and halved

4 carrots, scraped and quartered

1 large green pepper, quartered

60 ml (¼ cup) cooking oil

Wash the chicken thoroughly in cold water and drain in a colander. Marinate the chicken pieces in a mixture of salt, pepper, chilli powder, jeera, garlic and ginger paste, vinegar and Worcestershire sauce. Cover and set aside for 15 minutes.

To a large deep pot on medium heat, add the chicken pieces and water and boil for 25 minutes, or till all the water has cooked away. Steam the potatoes and carrots in a large pot on medium heat, till cooked but still firm. Add the green pepper to the chicken, placing the quarters between the chicken pieces, and then add the oil. Cook on medium heat till the chicken is nicely browned and cooked. Lastly, add the potatoes and carrots, stir through and cook on reduced heat for an additional 10–15 minutes. Remove from heat and serve.

CRUMBED CHICKEN

SERVE WITH ROLLS AND SALADS OR SAVOURY RICE, AND CREAMY MUSHROOM SAUCE.

SERVES 8–10

12–20 chicken pieces, skinned if preferred
250 ml (1 cup) water
10 ml (2 tsp) salt
10 ml (2 tsp) garlic and ginger paste
10 ml (2 tsp) Cajun spice
10 ml (2 tsp) garlic salt
10 ml (2 tsp) mother-in-law masala
5 ml (1 tsp) red leaf masala
5 ml (1 tsp) chilli powder
45 ml (3 Tbsp) mayonnaise
1 large egg, beaten
Breadcrumbs for coating
Cooking oil for deep-frying
Lettuce leaves, pineapple wedges and cocktail tomatoes for serving

Wash the chicken and pat dry with paper towel. Add the chicken pieces to a large pot, on medium heat. Add the water, 5 ml (1 tsp) salt and 5 ml (1 tsp) garlic and ginger paste, and allow to steam till the chicken is cooked. Drain the chicken pieces in a colander and blot off excess water with paper towel. Place the chicken pieces in a large mixing bowl and add the remaining salt and garlic and ginger paste, the Cajun spice, garlic salt, both masalas and chilli powder. Add the mayonnaise and beaten egg and mix through well, ensuring that all of the chicken is coated.

Dip the chicken pieces into the breadcrumbs, ensuring that each piece is coated. Place the chicken into a large dish and refrigerate for 1½ hours before frying. Place a large pot on medium heat, add enough oil for deep-frying and heat up. Just before frying, reduce heat slightly, place the chicken pieces into the oil, and slowly fry till golden brown. Remove from oil and drain on paper towel. Arrange the chicken pieces on a bed of lettuce and garnish with pineapple wedges and cocktail tomatoes.

Tip: To crumb chicken easily, place the breadcrumbs in a plastic bag, place each chicken portion into the bag, one at a time, and shake well. This method ensures even coating and is less messy.

MASALA TANDOORI CHICKEN

This is a popular, exotic Indian way of preparing chicken. It is usually served with naan bread and salads but can also be served with savoury rice or chips.

12–20 chicken pieces or 2 whole chickens, halved
20 ml (4 tsp) tandoori chicken masala
10 ml (2 tsp) red leaf masala
5 ml (1 tsp) ground jeera
2.5 ml (½ tsp) cayenne pepper
2.5 ml (½ tsp) turmeric
5 ml (1 tsp) chilli powder
5 ml (1 tsp) all-in-one masala
10 ml (2 tsp) salt, or to taste
10 ml (2 tsp) wet khokni masala
10 ml (2 tsp) garlic and ginger paste
125 ml (½ cup) cooking oil
15 ml (1 Tbsp) lemon juice
45 ml (3 Tbsp) fresh cream
30 ml (2 Tbsp) ghee or melted butter or margarine
1 medium pineapple, peeled and cut into wedges
Chopped fresh dhania for garnishing

SERVES 8–10

If preferred, remove the skin from the chicken. If using whole chickens, split them into four equal halves, between the legs, from the neck down through the centre. Wash the chicken pieces well with cold water and drain in a colander, blotting off excess water with paper towel. Slash the chicken pieces across each portion, ensuring not to cut too deeply. This will allow the spices to penetrate the meat and enhance the flavour. Mix all of the spices together with the garlic and ginger paste, 15 ml (1 Tbsp) of oil, the lemon juice and the cream. Rub the mixture onto the chicken, coating well. Cover and leave to stand for at least 1 hour.

Preheat the oven to 180 °C. Mix the remaining oil and ghee or melted butter together. Place the chicken pieces in a deep roasting pan, pour over half of the oil and butter mixture, and cover with foil, sealing it on the sides of the pan. Bake for about 45 minutes till done. Remove from the oven, remove the foil and place pineapple wedges between the chicken pieces. Pour over the remaining oil and butter mixture, and place, uncovered, directly under the grill for 5–10 minutes. Serve immediately, garnished with chopped dhania.

BUTTER CHICKEN

SERVES 6–8

THIS DISH IS OF INDIAN ORIGIN AND IS SERVED WITH NAAN BREAD OR ROTI AND A TOMATO AND ONION SALAD.

60 ml (¼ cup) cooking oil
2 cardamom pods
2.5 ml (½ tsp) jeera seeds
6 black peppercorns
1 fresh green chilli, finely chopped
2 medium onions, finely chopped
20 ml (4 tsp) garlic and ginger paste
800 g–1 kg chicken breasts, cubed
2 medium tomatoes, peeled and grated
5 ml (1 tsp) turmeric
10 ml (2 tsp) salt, or to taste
15 ml (1 Tbsp) ground jeera
15 ml (1 Tbsp) ground coriander
10 ml (2 tsp) cayenne pepper
5 ml (1 tsp) mother-in-law masala
5 ml (1 tsp) methi masala
125 ml (½ cup) plain yoghurt
15 ml (1 Tbsp) tomato paste
15 ml (1 Tbsp) sugar
250 ml (1 cup) fresh cream
60 ml (¼ cup) chopped fresh dhania

Place a large pot on medium heat, add the oil and heat. To this add the cardamom, jeera seeds, peppercorns, chilli and onions, and braise till lightly golden. Add the garlic and ginger paste and cubed chicken breasts, and stir and braise for about 8 minutes, or till lightly cooked. Add the grated tomatoes and all of the spices and stir to combine. Add the plain yoghurt, tomato paste and sugar, stir well and cook on reduced heat for about 15 minutes. Add the fresh cream and cook for a further 5–8 minutes. Lastly, sprinkle the chopped dhania on top – do not stir – and simmer for 5 minutes. Serve warm, as described above.

SWEET-AND-SOUR CHICKEN

SERVES 5–8

THIS RECIPE MAKES A DELICIOUS ANYTIME MEAL SERVED WITH COLD PASTA SALAD, BAKED POTATO AND ROLLS.

10–16 chicken pieces, skinned if preferred
7.5 ml (1½ tsp) tandoori chicken masala
10 ml (2 tsp) garlic salt
5 ml (1 tsp) salt, or to taste
5 ml (1 tsp) mother-in-law masala
5 ml (1 tsp) freshly ground black pepper
10 ml (2 tsp) crushed garlic
30 ml (2 Tbsp) Worcestershire sauce
30 ml (2 Tbsp) tomato sauce
15 ml (1 Tbsp) chutney
10 ml (2 tsp) golden syrup
125 ml (½ cup) water
60 ml (¼ cup) cooking oil

Wash the chicken pieces and then place them in a large mixing bowl. Add all of the spices, the garlic, sauces, chutney and syrup and mix through, coating all of the chicken. Leave to stand in the refrigerator for 15 minutes to marinate.

To a large pot on medium heat, add the marinated chicken pieces with the water. Cook for about 20 minutes, uncovered, or till most of the water has cooked away. Add the oil and cook on reduced heat for 15 minutes or till the chicken is completely cooked. Remove from heat and serve as described above.

CHICKEN AND POULTRY DISHES

CHICKEN TIKKA

SERVES 6–8

THIS MAKES A DELICIOUS LIGHT MEAL OR STARTER AND CAN BE SERVED WITH FRIED POTATO WEDGES AND SALADS.

800 g–1 kg chicken breasts, cubed
5 ml (1 tsp) salt, or to taste
10 ml (2 tsp) garlic and ginger paste
5 ml (1 tsp) ground jeera
2.5 ml (½ tsp) cayenne pepper
10 ml (2 tsp) chilli powder
15 ml (1 Tbsp) cooking oil
15 ml (1 Tbsp) lemon juice
1 large pineapple, peeled and cut into wedges
2 large red or green peppers, cut into wedges
30 ml (2 Tbsp) plain yoghurt
15 ml (1 Tbsp) mashed green pawpaw
30 ml (2 Tbsp) butter or margarine

Preheat the oven to 200 °C.

Wash the chicken and drain in a colander. Set aside.

Mix the salt, garlic and ginger paste and all the spices with the oil and lemon juice to form a paste. Coat the chicken cubes with the paste, making sure the cubes are well covered. Place the chicken on skewers, alternating the cubes with pineapple and green or red pepper wedges. Place the skewers in a large roasting pan.

Mix the yoghurt and mashed pawpaw together and pour the mixture over the skewers in the pan. Dot the skewers with some butter and place in the preheated oven for 15–20 minutes, or till done. Remove from the oven and serve as described above.

EID OVEN-ROASTED CHICKEN

SERVES 8–10

EVERYONE HAS THEIR OWN WAY OF PREPARING ROAST CHICKEN, BUT MY MOTHER'S RECIPE REMAINS THE BEST!

1.5–2 kg whole chicken
1 large onion, finely chopped
7 large potatoes, peeled and halved
25 ml (5 tsp) garlic and ginger paste
5 ml (1 tsp) salt, or to taste
5 ml (1 tsp) tandoori chicken masala
5 ml (1 tsp) red chilli paste
10 ml (2 tsp) ground coriander
10 ml (2 tsp) jeera seeds
60 ml (¼ cup) tamarind
60 ml (¼ cup) boiling water
10 ml (2 tsp) sugar
2 fresh green chillies, finely chopped
125 ml (½ cup) ghee/oil
2 pieces of stick cinnamon
5 cardamom pods
3 whole allspice
4 whole cloves

Preheat the oven to 180 °C. Wash and skin the chicken if preferred. Clean the cavity of the chicken well and allow to drain in a colander. Fry the onion in a little oil till lightly golden in colour. Remove from oil and drain in a colander. Set aside. Steam and then fry the potatoes till lightly golden. Set aside. Mix the garlic and ginger paste with the salt, tandoori chicken masala, chilli paste, coriander and jeera seeds, to form a paste. Divide the paste in two and set aside. Mix the tamarind with the boiling water and sugar and set aside. Add the chopped green chillies and fried onions to one half of the paste mixture. Mix well. Stuff this mixture into the cavity of the chicken, sealing the cavity with one or two fried potatoes. Smear the remaining paste all over the chicken. In a large pot, add the ghee or oil and heat along with the cinnamon, cardamom, allspice and cloves. Add the chicken and brown on all sides. Transfer the chicken to a roasting pan, pour over the tamarind mixture and roast, covered with foil, in the preheated oven for about 30 minutes. Remove from the oven, remove foil and arrange the potatoes around the chicken. Return to the oven, uncovered, for an additional 15–20 minutes, or till done. Serve with sweet yellow rice, a medley of vegetables and salads.

500–600 g puff pastry, to line and cover a standard size pie dish/tin

FILLING

60 ml (¼ cup) cooking oil
1 large onion, finely chopped
6 peppercorns
6 whole allspice
4 whole cloves
2.5 ml (½ tsp) jeera seeds
1 fresh green chilli, finely chopped
250 ml (1 cup) sliced mushrooms
1 small green pepper, finely chopped
125 ml (½ cup) whole kernel corn
7.5 ml (1½ tsp) salt, or to taste
5 ml (1 tsp) freshly ground black pepper
5 ml (1 tsp) red leaf masala
2.5 ml (½ tsp) tandoori chicken masala
60 ml (¼ cup) water
750 g chicken mince, or chicken breasts, cubed
60 ml (¼ cup) Worcestershire sauce
10 ml (2 tsp) garlic and ginger paste
60 ml (¼ cup) sago, soaked in 125 ml (½ cup) water for 8–10 minutes
1 large egg, beaten

Makes a delicious lunch or snack, served with salads.

SERVES 6

CHICKEN PIE

Preheat the oven to 180 °C. Heat the cooking oil in a medium-sized pot on medium heat. Add the onion along with the peppercorns, allspice, cloves and jeera seeds. Braise this onion mixture till golden brown. Now add the chopped chilli, the mushrooms, green pepper, corn, salt, black pepper, red leaf masala, tandoori masala and the water and simmer for about 5 minutes. Next, add the chicken along with the Worcestershire sauce, garlic and ginger paste and the sago. Simmer for about 20 minutes, stirring frequently. If the mixture becomes too dry, add about 15 ml (1 Tbsp) water and simmer till done, or till the sago becomes transparent. Remove from heat and allow to cool.

Roll out the pastry to about 5 mm thick and line the pie dish or tin. Fill with the chicken mixture and cover with another 5-mm-thick round of pastry, pressing the edges together to ensure the pie is sealed. Trim the edges, prick the top lightly with a fork and brush with beaten egg. Bake for 45 minutes, or till golden brown. Remove from the oven and serve as described above.

Meat dishes are popular with both Cape Malays and Indians. There are various ways in which they prepare their meat, from stews to curries and beyond.

MEAT DISHES

SOSATIE CHOPS

SERVES 6-8

THIS IS A FAVOURITE DISH AMONG THE CAPE MALAYS, AND IS SERVED WITH SWEET YELLOW RICE OR MASH, AND SALADS.

1 kg lamb leg chops
10 ml (2 tsp) salt, or to taste
60 ml (¼ cup) cooking oil
5 cardamom pods
3 pieces of stick cinnamon
5 ml (1 tsp) jeera seeds
6 black peppercorns
3 bay leaves
4 large onions, coarsely chopped
7.5 ml (1½ tsp) ground jeera
10 ml (2 tsp) red leaf masala
10 ml (2 tsp) all-in-one masala
7.5 ml (1½ tsp) turmeric
60 ml (¼ cup) brown vinegar
125 ml (½ cup) sugar
60 ml (¼ cup) water
60 ml (¼ cup) chopped fresh dhania

Clean the meat and remove the fat. Place the chops in a large pot of boiling water on medium heat, add 5 ml (1 tsp) salt and boil till the meat is tender. Remove the meat from the pot and drain in a colander. Set aside.

To a large pot on medium heat, add the oil and heat up. Add the cardamom, cinnamon, jeera seeds, peppercorns, bay leaves and onions. Braise for about 10 minutes or till lightly golden brown. Add all the spices, the remaining salt, the vinegar, sugar and water. Return the meat to the pot and stir through well. Simmer on reduced heat for about 10 minutes. Add the dhania and simmer for an additional 5 minutes, or till done. Remove from heat and serve as described above.

DENNING CHOPS

THIS DISH IS OF MALAY ORIGIN AND HAS A DELICIOUSLY DISTINCTIVE TASTE. IT IS SERVED WITH WHITE BRAISED RICE, MASH OR BAKED POTATO AND SALADS.

SERVES 6

1 kg lamb leg or loin chops
60 ml (¼ cup) cooking oil
6 whole allspice
6 black peppercorns
4 whole cloves
3 bay leaves
2 large onions, finely chopped
1 small green pepper, finely chopped
5 ml (1 tsp) garlic and ginger paste
10 ml (2 tsp) fine black pepper
60 ml (¼ cup) Worcestershire sauce
30 ml (2 Tbsp) brown vinegar
10 ml (2 tsp) salt, or to taste
250 ml (1 cup) water
2 large tomatoes, halved and grated
30 ml (2 Tbsp) sugar
2.5 ml (½ tsp) grated nutmeg

Wash the meat and remove the fat. Place in a colander to drain and set aside.

To a large pot on medium heat, add the oil and heat up. Add the allspice, peppercorns, cloves, bay leaves, onions and green pepper and braise till golden brown in colour. Add the meat, garlic and ginger paste, pepper, Worcestershire sauce, vinegar, salt and 200 ml (¾ cup) of the water and cook till all the water has cooked away and the meat is tender. Add the grated tomatoes, sugar and nutmeg with the remaining water, and simmer for 15–20 minutes, or till done. Remove from heat and serve as described above.

MEAT DISHES

This dish is usually served for Eid lunch among the Malay communities. The accompaniments would be sweet yellow rice, gem squash and salads.

1 leg of lamb (3–3.5 kg)
7.5 ml (1½ tsp) salt
45 ml (3 Tbsp) freshly ground black pepper
125 ml (½ cup) Worcestershire sauce
125 ml (½ cup) brown vinegar
10 ml (2 tsp) garlic and ginger paste
4 bay leaves
6 whole cloves
8 peppercorns
6 whole allspice
875 ml (3½ cups) water
7 large potatoes, peeled and halved
7 large carrots, scraped and halved
250 ml (1 cup) cooking oil

SERVES 8–10

POT ROAST LEG OF LAMB

Firstly, clean the leg thoroughly and remove all or most of the fat. Pat the leg dry and pierce different sections with a knife. This is to ensure that the leg cooks evenly and that the marinade gets absorbed into the meat. Place the leg in a large bowl and rub the entire leg with the salt and pepper, including the incisions in the meat.

Mix the Worcestershire sauce, vinegar and garlic and ginger paste together to form the marinade. Pour the marinade over the leg and rub into the meat. Add the bay leaves, cloves, peppercorns and allspice and mix well. Leave this to stand, covered, in the refrigerator for at least 6 hours or, ideally, overnight.

Place the leg in a large pot on high heat, and to this add the water. Cook for 1 hour, turning at 15-minute intervals till evenly cooked and the water has cooked away. The meat should be tender at this stage; if not, another cup of water can be added, and the leg cooked for an additional 10–15 minutes. Meanwhile, steam the potatoes and carrots in a pot on medium to high heat till cooked but still firm, and then drain and set aside. Once all the water has cooked away from the leg, add the oil, potatoes and carrots to the pot. Cook together for an additional 15–20 minutes. Remove from heat and serve as described above.

Note: If the roast sticks to the bottom of the pot at any time during the cooking process, add a little water and gently loosen and turn the leg while still cooking.

This is a simple meal to prepare, served with baked potato or fried potato wedges, salads and rolls. Alternatively, it can be served in pita pockets with tzatziki sauce and salads.

1 kg tenderized steak
10 ml (2 tsp) salt
10 ml (2 tsp) freshly ground black pepper
5 ml (1 tsp) garlic and ginger paste
2.5 ml (½ tsp) chilli powder
60 ml (¼ cup) Worcestershire sauce
60 ml (¼ cup) tomato sauce
250 ml (1 cup) water
60 ml (¼ cup) cooking oil
2 large onions, coarsely chopped
1 whole large fresh green chilli, slit in the centre

SERVES 6

BRAISED STEAK

Wash the steak and halve or, if you are preparing the steak for the pita pockets, cut the steak into bite-sized strips. Place the steak in a large mixing bowl and add the salt, black pepper, garlic and ginger paste, chilli powder, Worcestershire sauce and tomato sauce. Mix through, ensuring every piece of steak is coated with the marinade.

Place the steak in a pot on medium to high heat, add the water and cook till all the water has cooked away and the steak is tender. Add the oil, onions and whole chilli. Add an additional 60 ml (¼ cup) of water and simmer on medium heat for 5–10 minutes more. Remove from heat and serve as described above.

375 ml (1½ cups) plain yoghurt
¾ cucumber, peeled, seeded and coarsely chopped
2.5 ml (½ tsp) salt
2.5 ml (½ tsp) freshly ground black pepper
2.5 ml (½ tsp) cayenne pepper
1 fresh green chilli, finely chopped
2.5 ml (½ tsp) crushed garlic, or to taste (optional)

TZATZIKI SAUCE

Mix all of the sauce ingredients together.

Notes: For steak pita pockets, prepare in the same manner. Fill the pita pockets and drizzle tzatziki sauce in the opening, just before serving.

This tasty dish is served with sweet yellow rice or mashed potato, and beetroot salad.

1 kg steak mince	4 bay leaves
5 slices stale bread, crusts removed	2.5 ml (½ tsp) ground cloves
250 ml (1 cup) water	2 large eggs
45 ml (3 Tbsp) cooking oil	15 ml (1 Tbsp) lemon juice
1 medium onion, chopped	40 ml (8 tsp) sugar
10 ml (2 tsp) garlic paste	30 ml (2 Tbsp) butter or margarine
10 ml (2 tsp) salt	
10 ml (2 tsp) curry powder	**TOPPING**
5 ml (1 tsp) turmeric	2 large eggs, lightly beaten
5 ml (1 tsp) red leaf masala	20 ml (4 tsp) full-cream milk
2.5 ml (½ tsp) mother-in-law masala	

SERVES 6

BOBOTIE

Preheat the oven to 160 °C.

Wash and drain the mince and set aside.

Soak the bread in the water for 5 minutes, and then squeeze dry. Heat the oil in a large frying pan, add the onion and braise for 5–10 minutes till golden. Add the garlic paste, salt, curry powder, turmeric, red leaf masala, mother-in-law masala, bay leaves and ground cloves. Stir and simmer for 5 minutes. Place the drained mince into a mixing bowl along with the onion mixture, the eggs, lemon juice, bread, sugar and butter. Mix all of these ingredients thoroughly.

Spoon the mixture into a greased ovenproof dish and bake in the preheated oven for 40 minutes, or till golden brown. Remove from the oven, mix the topping ingredients together and pour over the bobotie. Return to the oven for a further 5–10 minutes at 180 °C, or till the topping is golden.

BRAISED CHOPS WITH TOMATO AND ONION

SERVES 6

THIS DISH IS QUICK AND EASY TO PREPARE AND CAN BE SERVED WITH WHITE RICE OR FRIED POTATO WEDGES, AND SALADS OR VEGGIES.

1 kg lamb leg or loin chops

10 ml (2 tsp) salt

10 ml (2 tsp) freshly ground black pepper

2.5 ml (½ tsp) chilli powder

5 ml (1 tsp) crushed garlic

250 ml (1 cup) water

6 peppercorns

5 whole allspice

60 ml (¼ cup) Worcestershire sauce

60 ml (¼ cup) cooking oil

2 medium onions, coarsely chopped

2 medium tomatoes, quartered (skin on)

Wash the chops and remove most of the fat. Place in a large mixing bowl. Add the salt, pepper, chilli powder and crushed garlic. Mix thoroughly, ensuring that every chop is well coated with the mixture.

To a large pot on medium to high heat, add the chops along with the water, peppercorns, allspice and Worcestershire sauce. Cook till all the water has cooked away. Add another 125 ml (½ cup) of water and cook for a further 10 minutes, till the water has cooked away and the meat is tender. Add the oil and simmer for 5 minutes. Now add the onions and simmer for an additional 5 minutes. Lastly, add the tomatoes along with 15 ml (1 Tbsp) of water and simmer for 10–15 minutes till done. Remove from heat and serve.

MASALA STEAK

SERVES 6

SERVE THESE TASTY STEAKS WITH NAAN ROLLS, CHIPS AND SALADS.

1 kg tenderized steak
10 ml (2 tsp) salt
10 ml (2 tsp) red leaf masala
5 ml (1 tsp) turmeric
5 ml (1 tsp) ground jeera
10 ml (2 tsp) mother-in-law masala
2.5 ml (½ tsp) all-in-one masala
2.5 ml (½ tsp) chilli powder
60 ml (¼ cup) tomato sauce
60 ml (¼ cup) Worcestershire sauce
60 ml (¼ cup) chopped fresh dhania
2.5 ml (½ tsp) garlic and ginger paste
1 fresh green chilli, slit midway
250 ml (1 cup) water
125 ml (½ cup) cooking oil
2 medium onions, coarsely chopped

Wash and drain the steak. Place the steak in a large bowl and add the salt, all of the spices, the tomato sauce, Worcestershire sauce, chopped dhania, garlic and ginger paste and the fresh chilli. Mix through well, coating all of the chops in the mixture.

Place the steaks and water in a pot on medium heat and cook till the meat is tender and the water has cooked away. If the steaks are not tender at this stage, add an extra 60 ml (¼ cup) of water and simmer for a further 5–10 minutes. Add the oil and the onions and braise for 10–15 minutes. Remove from heat and serve.

These kebabs are usually served with sweet yellow rice or fried potato wedges, and green bean bajie. They make a great meal and are quite simple to prepare.

1 kg steak mince
22.5 ml (1½ Tbsp) cooking oil
1 large onion, finely chopped
1 medium fresh green chilli, finely chopped
6 black peppercorns
5 whole cloves
5 whole allspice
2.5 ml (½ tsp) chilli powder
5 ml (1 tsp) red leaf masala
5 ml (1 tsp) turmeric
10 ml (2 tsp) garlic and ginger paste
1 large egg
2.5 ml (½ tsp) salt, or to taste
60 ml (¼ cup) chopped fresh dhania
5 slices stale bread
3 hard-boiled eggs, quartered

MAKES 12

MINCE KEBABS

Wash and drain the mince in a colander and set aside. Add the oil to a large frying pan and heat. Add the onion, green chilli, peppercorns, cloves and allspice. Braise till the onion is golden brown in colour. Add the chilli powder, red leaf masala and turmeric, and stir well. Simmer on medium heat for 5 minutes. Remove from heat and allow to cool. Remove and discard the peppercorns, allspice and cloves.

Place the mince in a large mixing bowl and add the garlic and ginger paste, egg, salt and dhania. Soak the bread in water for 2 minutes, then remove and squeeze out the excess water. Add the bread to the mince along with the onion mixture. Mix thoroughly, combining all of the ingredients.

Take a tablespoonful of mixture and flatten it in the palm of your hand. Place an egg quarter in the middle and cover firmly with mince, patting it into the shape of an egg. Repeat till the mince mixture is used up. Deep-fry in hot oil till evenly browned. Drain on paper towel and serve as described above.

TRADITIONAL CORNED BEEF

SERVES 6-8

CORNED BEEF IS USUALLY SERVED WITH ROLLS AND SALADS ON EID MORNINGS.

1 kg topside beef
22.5 ml (1½ Tbsp) salt
7.5 ml (1½ tsp) fine black pepper
4 bay leaves
6 whole cloves
8 peppercorns
60 ml (¼ cup) Worcestershire sauce
1.5 litres (6 cups) water

Wash the meat well and make random slits with a sharp knife, about 2 cm deep. Place the meat in a mixing bowl. Rub with all of the salt and black pepper. Insert the bay leaves, cloves and peppercorns into the slits in the meat. Pour the Worcestershire sauce over and rub it into the meat, making sure it is well covered. Marinate, covered, in the refrigerator overnight.

The following morning, place the meat in a large saucepan, add the water and simmer on medium heat for about 2 hours, or till done. Turn occasionally during the cooking process. Serve as described above.

CREAMY PEPPER STEAK

SERVES 6–8

A CREAMY, MILDLY SPICED STEAK DISH SERVED WITH BRAISED WHITE RICE OR FRIED POTATO WEDGES, AND SALADS.

800 g steak of choice, cut into bite-sized cubes
60 ml (¼ cup) melted butter
60 ml (¼ cup) cooking oil
6 black peppercorns
4 whole allspice
3 whole cloves
3 medium onions, finely chopped
1 medium green pepper, chopped
1 whole fresh green chilli, slit open
10 ml (2 tsp) garlic and ginger paste
30 ml (2 Tbsp) water
1 x 250 g punnet button mushrooms, sliced
7.5 ml (1½ tsp) salt, or to taste
7.5 ml (1½ tsp) fine black pepper
5 ml (1 tsp) mother-in-law masala
2.5 ml (½ tsp) cayenne pepper
20 ml (4 tsp) white sugar
250 ml (1 cup) fresh cream
1 x 415 g tin cream of mushroom soup
60 ml (¼ cup) chopped fresh dhania

Wash the steak cubes and drain in a colander. To a large pot on medium to high heat, add the butter and cooking oil and heat. Once it starts to sizzle, add the peppercorns, allspice, cloves, onions, green pepper and chilli. Braise on medium heat till the onions are golden brown. Add the steak cubes along with the garlic and ginger paste. Immediately add the water and stir. Cook for 15 minutes, or till the steak cubes are tender.

Next, add the mushrooms, salt, black pepper, mother-in-law masala, cayenne pepper and sugar. Stir and simmer for 5 minutes. Add the cream and the mushroom soup and cook, uncovered, for 15 minutes. Lastly, add the chopped dhania and simmer on low heat for 10 minutes. Remove from heat and serve.

Curries are very popular with both Malay and Indian communities. Malay curries are usually sweeter than the Indian curries, which are stronger and bolder in taste.

CURRIES AND BREYANIS

The curry recipes in this chapter are a fusion of the two, which gives them that extra twist. Breyani is a spiced, layered rice dish with either meat, chicken or seafood, and is served with dhai or sambals.

1 kg fish, washed and portioned
60 ml (¼ cup) cooking oil
15 ml (1 Tbsp) butter or margarine
2.5 ml (½ tsp) jeera seeds
1 ml (¼ tsp) methi seeds
2.5 ml (½ tsp) black mustard seeds
6 curry leaves
6 black peppercorns
2 large onions, finely chopped
10 ml (2 tsp) garlic and ginger paste
10 ml (2 tsp) fish masala
5 ml (1 tsp) salt
5 ml (1 tsp) turmeric
2.5 ml (½ tsp) chilli powder
7.5 ml (1½ tsp) red leaf masala
2 medium tomatoes, peeled and grated
125 ml (½ cup) coconut milk (optional)
10 ml (2 tsp) tomato paste
60 ml (¼ cup) chopped fresh dhania

This is a tangy, mild curry that is served with braised white rice and sambals. Any type of fish may be used for this recipe, provided that it is firm and not too flaky.

SERVES 6

FISH CURRY

Pat dry the fish portions and set aside.

Place a medium-sized pot on medium to high heat, add the oil and butter, and allow the butter to melt. Add the jeera, methi and mustard seeds along with the curry leaves and peppercorns. Add the onions and braise for 10 minutes till golden. Add the garlic and ginger paste and all the spices and stir thoroughly. Add the grated tomatoes, stir to combine and simmer for 5 minutes on medium heat. Next, add the coconut milk and tomato paste. Stir and simmer on medium heat for a further 5 minutes. Add the fish portions and mix through gently. Cook for 15 minutes on low heat till done. Lastly, add the dhania and simmer 5 minutes longer. Remove from heat and serve.

Variation: For a sweet/spicy variation, add 15 ml (1 Tbsp) white sugar to the curry during the cooking process. This applies to all curry recipes.

This recipe is so versatile, one can substitute the mutton with fish, chicken or prawns if desired. Mutton curry is usually served with roti and tomato and onion sambal, or with white rice.

60 ml (¼ cup) cooking oil
15 ml (1 Tbsp) butter or margarine
3 pieces of stick cinnamon
4 cardamom pods
4 whole cloves
4 whole allspice
5 ml (1 tsp) jeera seeds
2.5 ml (½ tsp) methi seeds
3 large onions, chopped
1 kg lamb or mutton pieces
10 ml (2 tsp) garlic and ginger paste
7.5 ml (1½ tsp) salt
30 ml (1 Tbsp) water
5 potatoes, peeled and cut into thirds
2 medium tomatoes, peeled and grated
1 fresh green chilli, slit midway
5 ml (1 tsp) red leaf masala
7.5 ml (1½ tsp) mother-in-law masala
5 ml (1 tsp) turmeric
2.5 ml (½ tsp) chilli powder
2.5 ml (½ tsp) wet khokni masala
5 ml (1 tsp) ground coriander
5 ml (1 tsp) ground jeera
2.5 ml (½ tsp) methi masala
125 ml (½ cup) coconut milk
60 ml (¼ cup) chopped fresh dhania

SERVES 6–8

MUTTON CURRY

Place a large pot on medium to high heat. Add the oil and butter. Once the butter has melted, add the cinnamon, cardamom, cloves, allspice and jeera and methi seeds. Add the onions and braise till lightly golden in colour. Add the washed meat, garlic and ginger paste and salt. Add the water and cook for 15–20 minutes till the meat is cooked.

Meanwhile, place the potatoes in a pot of water with a pinch of salt added and steam till cooked but still firm. Drain. In another pot on medium to high heat, add enough oil to fry the potatoes and heat. Add the potatoes and fry till golden.

To the pot of meat, add the grated tomatoes, the whole chilli and all of the spices, and simmer for 5 minutes. Add the coconut milk and stir. Simmer for an additional 5 minutes before adding the fried potatoes. Lastly, add the chopped dhania and simmer slowly for 10 minutes till done. Remove from heat and serve warm as described above.

This is a very popular dish among both Indians and Malays. Serve with white rice or roti and sambals.

KALYA CHICKEN CURRY

1.5 kg chicken pieces (thigh, drumstick, breast, wing)
60 ml (¼ cup) cooking oil
2 large onions, coarsely chopped
4 cardamom pods
3 pieces of stick cinnamon
10 ml (2 tsp) jeera seeds
2.5 ml (½ tsp) mustard seeds
1 star anise
6 potatoes, peeled and halved
7.5 ml (1½ tsp) garlic and ginger paste
60 ml (¼ cup) water
3 large tomatoes, peeled and grated
10 ml (2 tsp) red leaf masala
5 ml (1 tsp) mother-in-law masala
10 ml (2 tsp) tandoori chicken masala
5 ml (1 tsp) turmeric
5 ml (1 tsp) ground jeera
2.5 ml (½ tsp) chilli powder or 5 ml (1 tsp) for a stronger curry
10 ml (2 tsp) salt, or to taste
125 ml (½ cup) coconut milk
5–6 curry leaves
60 ml (¼ cup) chopped fresh dhania

SERVES 6–8

Wash and skin the chicken portions and set aside. Heat the cooking oil in a large pot on high heat. Reduce to medium heat and add the onions, cardamom, cinnamon, jeera seeds, mustard seeds and star anise. Braise till lightly golden brown. Meanwhile, steam the potatoes in a little water with salt to taste, till cooked but still firm. Drain and set aside.

Add the chicken pieces to the pot with the onions. Add the garlic and ginger paste and water and simmer for 10 minutes. Next, add the grated tomatoes, red leaf masala, mother-in-law masala, tandoori chicken masala, turmeric, ground jeera, chilli powder, salt, coconut milk and curry leaves. Stir well, making sure all of the ingredients are combined. Cook for 10–15 minutes. Tuck the potatoes between the chicken pieces and stir, ensuring the potatoes are covered with gravy. Lastly, add the dhania and simmer for 5 minutes. Remove from heat and serve.

Note: The coconut milk can be substituted with 60 ml (¼ cup) full-cream milk mixed with 7.5 ml (1½ tsp) lemon juice. Leave this mixture to stand for 10 minutes before using. This recipe can be varied by replacing the chicken with any other meat, such as fish or mutton.

*A favourite dish to serve for Eid lunch.
It can be served with white rice or
Indian puri and salads.*

8 medium crayfish tails	2 large tomatoes, peeled and grated
125 ml (½ cup) ghee	10 ml (2 tsp) garlic and ginger paste
2 large onions, chopped	10 ml (2 tsp) salt, or to taste
4 cardamom pods, split open	125 ml (½ cup) coconut milk (optional)
3 pieces of stick cinnamon	7.5 ml (1½ tsp) red leaf masala
6 whole allspice	7.5 ml (1½ tsp) mother-in-law masala
5 whole cloves	10 ml (2 tsp) seafood masala
6 curry leaves	5 ml (1 tsp) wet khokni masala
6 peppercorns	5 ml (1 tsp) turmeric
5 ml (1 tsp) jeera seeds	5 ml (1 tsp) white sugar
5 ml (1 tsp) mustard seeds	60 ml (¼ cup) water
1 star anise	60 ml (¼ cup) chopped fresh dhania
1 whole fresh green chilli, slit open	

SERVES 6–8

CRAYFISH TAIL CURRY

Slit the crayfish tails through the centre, on the underside, and remove the vein. Cut each tail into three equal portions and wash under cold running water. Drain in a colander and set aside. To a large pot on medium heat, add the ghee and heat. To this, add the onions, cardamom pods, cinnamon, allspice, cloves, curry leaves, peppercorns, jeera seeds, mustard seeds and star anise and braise till the onions are golden brown in colour. Next, add the whole green chilli, grated tomatoes, garlic and ginger paste, salt and coconut milk, if using, and simmer for 5–10 minutes.

Add all of the spices, the sugar and water and stir to combine. Simmer for an additional 8 minutes. If the gravy becomes too thick add 15 ml (1 Tbsp) of water during cooking. Add the crayfish tails to the pot and stir to ensure the tails are covered in the sauce. Cook on medium heat for 8 minutes, or till done (when the meat is white, tender but still firm). Lastly, add the chopped dhania and simmer on low heat for 5 minutes. Remove from heat and serve.

Note: The coconut milk is optional and can be omitted. Clarified butter can be substituted by melting 1 part butter (not margarine) to 2 parts cooking oil.

Fragrant and spicy, this curry also has a dash of sweetness. It can be served with either roti or white braised rice, or kitchri rice and salads.

1 kg pumpkin, peeled and cubed
750 g chicken breasts, cubed
125 ml (½ cup) ghee or
60 ml (¼ cup) cooking oil
2 large onions, finely chopped
2.5 ml (½ tsp) methi seeds
2.5 ml (½ tsp) mustard seeds
6 peppercorns
7.5 ml (1½ tsp) garlic and ginger paste
10 ml (2 tsp) red leaf masala
5 ml (1 tsp) ground jeera
5 ml (1 tsp) turmeric
60 ml (¼ cup) water
10 ml (2 tsp) salt, or to taste
30 ml (2 Tbsp) white sugar
2.5 ml (½ tsp) crushed dried red chillies
1 small fresh green chilli, finely chopped
60 ml (¼ cup) desiccated coconut
60 ml (¼ cup) chopped fresh dhania

SERVES 6–8

PUMPKIN CURRY

Wash the pumpkin pieces and place in a pot with enough water to cover, and boil till soft. Drain in a colander and set aside. Wash the chicken breast cubes, drain in a colander and set aside.

To a large pot on medium to high heat, add the ghee or cooking oil and heat up. Once the ghee or oil sizzles, add the onions along with the methi seeds, mustard seeds and peppercorns. Braise till lightly golden. Reduce the heat to medium and add the garlic and ginger paste. Simmer for 2 minutes. Next, add the cubed chicken and simmer for 5 minutes.

Add the red leaf masala, ground jeera, turmeric, water, salt, sugar, crushed red chillies and chopped green chilli and simmer for about 5 minutes. Next, add the pumpkin cubes and simmer for 10 minutes. Add 15 ml (1 Tbsp) water during the cooking process if the mixture becomes too dry. Meanwhile, place the coconut in a pan on medium heat and dry-fry till golden brown in colour. Immediately sprinkle the coconut and chopped dhania over the pumpkin mixture, and simmer on medium to low heat for 5–8 minutes. Remove from heat and serve as described above.

MUTTON DHAL CURRY

SERVES 6–8

THE NUTRITIOUS RED LENTILS GIVE THIS CURRY ADDED SUBSTANCE.

500 g red lentils (dhal)

1 kg mutton pieces or stewing meat

2 medium onions, finely chopped

2 pieces of stick cinnamon

5 cardamom pods, split open

6 black peppercorns

4 whole cloves

2.5 ml (½ tsp) jeera seeds

10 ml (2 tsp) garlic and ginger paste

1 whole fresh green chilli, slit

250 ml (1 cup) water

60 ml (¼ cup) cooking oil

2 large tomatoes, peeled and grated

10 ml (2 tsp) red leaf masala

5 ml (1 tsp) turmeric

5 ml (1 tsp) wet khokni masala

5 ml (1 tsp) mutton masala

2.5 ml (½ tsp) salt, or to taste

60 ml (¼ cup) chopped fresh dhania

Firstly, cook the lentils in sufficient water till all the water has cooked away and the lentils are completely soft and form a paste. Remove from heat and set aside. To a medium-sized pot on medium heat, add the mutton pieces, onions, cinnamon, cardamom, peppercorns, cloves, jeera seeds, garlic and ginger paste and whole chilli. Add the water, stir well and cook for 10–15 minutes till the meat is tender and the water has cooked away. If the meat is not tender enough at this stage, add an additional 60 ml (¼ cup) of water and cook for a further 8–10 minutes. Add the cooking oil and simmer for 5 minutes. Add the grated tomatoes along with all of the spices and salt. Stir and simmer on medium heat for 5–8 minutes.

Add the cooked lentils and stir well, combining all of the ingredients. If the mixture is too thick at this stage, you can add an extra 60 ml (¼ cup) of water. Simmer on medium to low heat for 10 minutes. Lastly, add the chopped dhania and simmer for an additional 2 minutes. Remove from heat and serve with warm rotis and a tomato and onion salad. This dish may also be served with white rice.

Variation: The meat in this recipe may be substituted with chicken pieces. Omit the mutton masala and add 5 ml (1 tsp) tandoori chicken masala instead. Cook in exactly the same manner.

MAFFROU

SERVES 8-10

THIS DISH IS SIMILAR TO AKHNI AND IS ALSO A FAVOURITE TO SERVE AT INDIAN WEDDINGS.

- 1 kg steak, cut into bite-sized cubes
- 1 whole fresh green chilli, slit open
- 125 ml (½ cup) buttermilk
- 12.5 ml (2½ tsp) salt, or to taste
- 10 ml (2 tsp) garlic and ginger paste
- 6 curry leaves
- 10 ml (2 tsp) red leaf masala
- 5 ml (1 tsp) chilli powder
- 5 ml (1 tsp) ground jeera
- 10 ml (2 tsp) mother-in-law masala
- 5 ml (1 tsp) turmeric
- 5 ml (1 tsp) wet khokni masala
- 2.5 ml (½ tsp) ground coriander
- 125 ml (½ cup) chopped fresh dhania
- 125 ml (½ cup) ghee or 60 ml (¼ cup) oil
- 2 large onions, finely chopped
- 5 cardamom pods, split open
- 2 pieces of stick cinnamon
- 5 ml (1 tsp) jeera seeds
- 2.5 ml (½ tsp) mustard seeds
- 125 ml (½ cup) water
- 6 hard-boiled eggs, halved

Wash the steak cubes, drain in a colander and transfer to a large mixing bowl. Add the whole chilli, buttermilk, salt, garlic and ginger paste, curry leaves, red leaf masala, chilli powder, ground jeera, mother-in-law masala, turmeric, khokni masala, ground coriander and dhania. Mix all of these ingredients well and set aside to marinate for 25–30 minutes. Place the ghee or oil in a large pot on medium to high heat and, once hot, add the onions, cardamom, cinnamon, jeera seeds and mustard seeds. Braise till the onions are golden brown in colour. Next, add the steak, marinade and water to the pot and cook on medium heat for 15–20 minutes till the steak cubes are tender and cooked. Reduce to low heat and simmer for a further 10 minutes till the oil has risen to the top. This will indicate that the dish is ready to be served. Spoon the meat mixture onto a serving platter and arrange the halved eggs between the meat, allowing them to soak in the gravy. Garnish with a sprinkle of chopped dhania and serve with white or kitchri rice and fried potato wedges.

MUTTON AKHNI

This is a traditional dish often served at weddings, with salads and dhai. Dhai is a spiced yoghurt or buttermilk-based sauce and is always served as an accompaniment to both akhni and breyani dishes.

1 kg mutton pieces
6 medium potatoes, peeled and halved
1 heaped tsp of saffron (optional)
250 ml (1 cup) boiling water
3 large onions, finely chopped
15 ml (1 Tbsp) butter or margarine
250 ml (1 cup) buttermilk
1 large whole fresh green chilli, slit open
15 ml (1 Tbsp) garlic and ginger paste
125 ml (½ cup) chopped fresh dhania
12.5 ml (2½ tsp) salt, or to taste
12.5 ml (2½ tsp) red leaf masala
10 ml (2 tsp) ground jeera
5 ml (1 tsp) chilli powder
10 ml (2 tsp) mother-in-law masala
10 ml (2 tsp) wet khokni masala
10 ml (2 tsp) turmeric
1 kg basmati rice
250 ml (1 cup) ghee
7.5 ml (1½ tsp) jeera seeds
5 ml (1 tsp) mustard seeds
2 bay leaves
6 cardamom pods, split open
4 pieces of stick cinnamon
60 ml (¼ cup) water

SERVES 8–10

Wash the mutton pieces, drain and set aside. Boil the potatoes in a little water, with salt to taste, till half-cooked and still firm. Infuse the saffron in the boiling water and set aside. Pan-fry 1 chopped onion in 15 ml (1 Tbsp) of the butter and set aside.

Place the mutton pieces in a large mixing bowl and add the buttermilk, green chilli, garlic and ginger paste, dhania, salt, red leaf masala, ground jeera, chilli powder, mother-in-law masala, wet khokni masala and turmeric. Mix thoroughly, ensuring that all of the mutton pieces are covered in the marinade. Set aside for 1 hour.

Rinse the rice in a colander, drain and place in a large pot on medium to high heat. Add water to reach halfway and add 45 ml (3 Tbsp) salt. Boil till half-cooked (the rice grains should be firm). Transfer to a colander and rinse under cold running water. Drain and set aside.

To a large pot on medium to high heat, add the ghee and heat. Add the remaining chopped onions along with the jeera seeds, mustard seeds, bay leaves, cardamom pods and cinnamon and braise till golden in colour. Add the marinated mutton pieces along with the marinade, the 60 ml (¼ cup) of water and simmer on medium heat for about 30 minutes, or till the meat is tender and cooked.

Arrange the potatoes between the mutton pieces and spoon the rice directly on top. Pour the fried onion with the melted butter over the rice, and lastly pour the cup of water containing the saffron over the rice and onions. Steam, covered, for 35 minutes. Remove from heat and serve with dhai and a tomato and onion salad.

Note: All akhnis and breyanis should be dished from the bottom up.

Variation: The mutton may be substituted with chicken pieces (thigh, drumstick, wing and breast) and prepared in exactly the same manner. Note that the breast portion should be halved.

For this dish, one can either use mixed frozen seafood or prawns and crayfish tails, depending on preference. Serve with dhai, tomato and onion salad, poppadoms and fried potato wedges.

750 ml (3 cups) basmati rice
125 ml (½ cup) ghee or 60 ml (¼ cup) cooking oil
2 large onions, finely chopped
1 whole fresh green chilli, slit open
5 ml (1 tsp) jeera seeds
2.5 ml (½ tsp) mustard seeds
6 black peppercorns
60 ml (¼ cup) water
125 ml (½ cup) coconut milk
10 ml (2 tsp) red leaf masala
10 ml (2 tsp) wet khokni masala
5 ml (1 tsp) turmeric
2.5 ml (½ tsp) chilli powder
2.5 ml (½ tsp) mother-in-law masala
5 ml (1 tsp) seafood masala
10 ml (2 tsp) garlic and ginger paste
12.5 ml (2½ tsp) salt, or to taste
125 ml (½ cup) chopped fresh dhania
1 kg frozen/fresh mixed seafood or 750 g prawns and 6 crayfish tails

SERVES 6–8

SEAFOOD AKHNI

NOTE: IF USING PRAWNS AND CRAYFISH TAILS, THE PRAWNS SHOULD BE SHELLED AND DEVEINED; THE CRAYFISH TAILS SHOULD BE CUT INTO THREE PORTIONS, SLIT THROUGH AND DEVEINED.

Rinse the rice in a colander under cold running water. Drain and transfer to a large pot on medium to high heat. Add water till half full, along with 15 ml (1 Tbsp) salt, and boil till half-cooked (the rice grains should be firm). Transfer the rice to a colander and rinse under cold running water. Drain and set aside.

To a large pot on medium to high heat, add the ghee or oil and heat. Once the ghee starts to sizzle, reduce to medium heat and add the onions, green chilli, jeera seeds, mustard seeds and peppercorns. Braise till the onions are golden brown in colour. Next, add the water, coconut milk, red leaf masala, khokni masala, turmeric, chilli powder, mother-in-law masala, seafood masala and garlic and ginger paste. Stir and simmer for 15 minutes. Add the salt and dhania and stir to combine all of the ingredients. Simmer for 5 minutes, then add the seafood and cook for 10–15 minutes. Lastly, add the drained rice and mix thoroughly, ensuring that the rice is coated with the gravy. Steam, covered, on low heat for 10–15 minutes more. Remove from heat and serve.

1 kg mutton pieces	10 ml (2 tsp) saffron
375 ml (1½ cups) buttermilk	125 ml (½ cup) boiling water
1 whole fresh green chilli, slit open	7 large potatoes, peeled and halved
10 ml (2 tsp) salt, or to taste	750 g basmati rice
15 ml (1 Tbsp) garlic and ginger paste	400 g brown lentils
10 ml (2 tsp) red leaf masala	60 ml (¼ cup) cooking oil
10 ml (2 tsp) all-in-one masala	200 g butter
10 ml (2 tsp) wet khokni masala	3 large onions, finely chopped
10 ml (2 tsp) turmeric	4 pieces of stick cinnamon
10 ml (2 tsp) ground jeera	6 cardamom pods, split open
5 ml (1 tsp) ground coriander	3 bay leaves
5 ml (1 tsp) chilli powder	5 ml (1 tsp) jeera seeds
2.5 ml (½ tsp) methi masala	2.5 ml (½ tsp) mustard seeds
60 ml (¼ cup) chopped fresh dhania	1 large onion, coarsely chopped for garnishing

SERVES 8–10

MUTTON BREYANI

Wash the mutton pieces and drain in a colander. Transfer to a large mixing bowl. Add the buttermilk, green chilli, salt, garlic and ginger paste, red leaf masala, all-in-one masala, khokni masala, turmeric, ground jeera, ground coriander, chilli powder, methi masala, dhania and 5 ml (1 tsp) saffron strands. Mix thoroughly. Let this stand for about 30 minutes. Infuse the remaining saffron in the boiling water and set aside. Steam the potato halves in a little water in a separate pot till slightly soft, then deep-fry till golden brown. Set aside. Rinse the rice and transfer to a pot filled to halfway with water. Add 15 ml (1 Tbsp) salt and boil till half-cooked and the rice grains are semi-soft. Rinse the rice in a colander, drain and set aside. Cook the lentils in a separate pot till semi-soft but not mushy. Drain and set aside.

To a large pot on high heat, add the oil and 60 g of the butter and, once it starts to sizzle, add the 3 chopped onions, cinnamon, cardamom, bay leaves, jeera seeds and mustard seeds. Braise till golden brown in colour. Add the meat mixture along with the marinade to the braised onions and cook for about 20 minutes, or till the meat is tender and the oil rises to the top. Next, add the cooked lentils, stir and arrange the potatoes between the pieces of meat. Spread the rice all over the top of the meat mixture and pour the 125 ml (½ cup) of the water containing the saffron on top of the rice. Pan-fry the coarsely chopped onion in the remaining butter till golden brown. Pour this over the rice, cover and steam for 30–35 minutes on low heat. Remove from heat and serve.

Variation: For Chicken Breyani, replace the mutton with skinned chicken pieces, and prepare in exactly the same manner.

Bredies and stews are subtly spiced with a hint of sweetness, simmered to perfection and served mainly with white rice, making a perfect and nutritious everyday meal.

BREDIES AND STEWS

PUMPKIN BREDIE

SERVES 6

PUMPKIN BREDIE IS BEST SERVED WITH PLAIN WHITE RICE OR THE BRAISED VARIATION, AND CAN BE ENJOYED AT SUPPER OR LUNCH TIME.

1 kg pumpkin, peeled and cubed
1 kg mutton pieces
2 large onions, finely chopped
250 ml (1 cup) water
5 ml (1 tsp) garlic and ginger paste
10 ml (2 tsp) salt, or to taste
2 pieces of stick cinnamon
1 star anise
4 whole allspice
6 peppercorns
60 ml (¼ cup) cooking oil
3 large tomatoes, peeled and grated
5 ml (1 tsp) chilli powder
2.5 ml (½ tsp) turmeric
15 ml (1 Tbsp) white sugar
60 ml (¼ cup) Worcestershire sauce

In a medium-sized pot over medium to high heat, boil the pumpkin in a little water till cooked but still firm (the pumpkin should hold its shape and not be too soft).

Wash the mutton pieces and drain in a colander. To a large pot on medium heat, add the meat along with the onions, water, garlic and ginger paste, salt, cinnamon, star anise, allspice and peppercorns. Boil for about 15 minutes till the meat is tender and all of the water has cooked away. If the meat is not tender enough, add an additional 60 ml (¼ cup) of water and cook for 10 minutes more. Next, add the cooking oil and simmer for 5 minutes. Add the grated tomatoes, chilli powder, turmeric, sugar and Worcestershire sauce. Stir to combine all of the ingredients and simmer for 10 minutes. Add the cooked pumpkin cubes, stir gently and simmer for an additional 10 minutes on low heat. Remove from heat and serve with white rice and atchar.

CABBAGE BREDIE

SERVES 6–8

THIS IS A REAL TREAT ON COLD WINTER DAYS AND IS BEST SERVED WITH PLAIN WHITE RICE AND ATCHAR.

1 kg stewing meat or mutton pieces
2 large onions, chopped
6 whole allspice
4 whole cloves
2 bay leaves
5 ml (1 tsp) garlic and ginger paste
10 ml (2 tsp) salt, or to taste
250 ml (1 cup) water
60 ml (¼ cup) cooking oil
3 large tomatoes, peeled and grated
2.5 ml (½ tsp) chilli powder
10 ml (2 tsp) white sugar
1 ml (¼ tsp) turmeric
5 ml (1 tsp) fine black pepper
1 whole fresh green chilli, slit open
60 ml (¼ cup) Worcestershire sauce
1 cabbage, cut into 1-cm-thick ribbons
5 large potatoes, peeled and halved

Wash the meat and drain in a colander. To a large pot on medium to high heat, add the meat along with the onions, allspice, cloves, bay leaves, garlic and ginger paste, salt and water. Let this cook for 15 minutes on medium heat till the meat is tender and all the water has cooked away. Add the cooking oil and simmer for 5 minutes. Next, add the grated tomatoes along with the chilli powder, sugar, turmeric, black pepper, green chilli and Worcestershire sauce. Stir to combine all of the ingredients and simmer for 10 minutes on low heat. Add the cabbage ribbons, stir and simmer for 20 minutes till the cabbage is cooked. Add 15 ml (1 Tbsp) water during the cooking process if the bredie becomes too dry.

Meanwhile, in a separate pot, boil the potatoes in a little water with 5 ml (1 tsp) salt till the potatoes are cooked but still firm. Add the drained potatoes to the bredie and stir to combine. Simmer, covered, on a low heat for about 10 minutes. Remove from heat and serve.

BREDIES AND STEWS

TOMATO FRIKKADEL BREDIE

This bredie was always my favourite as a child, and is best served with plain white rice. Leftover bredie can also be enjoyed with your favourite pasta.

SERVES 8–10

FRIKKADELS

- 1 kg steak mince
- 1 large egg
- 60 ml (¼ cup) chopped fresh dhania
- 10 ml (2 tsp) salt, or to taste
- 10 ml (2 tsp) dried parsley
- 10 ml (2 tsp) fine black pepper
- 5 ml (1 tsp) red leaf masala
- 2.5 ml (½ tsp) chilli powder
- 10 ml (2 tsp) crushed garlic
- 4 slices of stale white bread
- 1 large onion, finely chopped
- 1 fresh green chilli, finely chopped

Wash and drain the mince in a colander, making sure all of the excess water has been drained. Place the mince in a large mixing bowl and add the egg, dhania, salt, parsley, black pepper, red leaf masala, chilli powder and crushed garlic. Soak the bread in cold water for 2 minutes. Remove and squeeze the excess water from the bread. Add the bread to the mince mixture. Add the onion and chilli and mix all of the ingredients together, making sure everything is combined. Take tablespoonsful of the mince mixture and roll into egg-shaped rounds. Leave to stand in the refrigerator for 20 minutes. Fry the frikkadels in shallow oil till evenly browned. Drain on paper towel and set aside.

TOMATO GRAVY

- 60 ml (¼ cup) cooking oil
- 6 peppercorns
- 4 whole allspice
- 3 large onions, finely chopped
- 4 medium tomatoes, peeled and grated
- 60 ml (¼ cup) water
- 10 ml (2 tsp) salt, or to taste
- 5 ml (1 tsp) red leaf masala
- 2.5 ml (½ tsp) chilli powder
- 5 ml (1 tsp) garlic and ginger paste
- 60 ml (¼ cup) white sugar
- 1 x 70 g tin tomato paste

Place a large pot on high heat, add the oil and heat. Once the oil starts to sizzle, reduce heat to medium and add the peppercorns and allspice. Add the onions and braise till golden brown. Add the grated tomatoes and simmer for 5 minutes. Next, add the water, salt, red leaf masala, chilli powder, garlic and ginger paste, sugar and tomato paste. Stir and simmer on medium heat for 15 minutes, adding an additional 60 ml (¼ cup) of water during cooking if the stew becomes too thick.

Place all the frikkadels in the tomato gravy and stir gently. Simmer, covered, on low heat for 10 minutes. Remove from heat and serve with white rice or fried potato wedges.

CARROTS AND PEAS STEW

SERVES 6-8

THIS IS A FAVOURITE DISH AMONG THE MALAYS AND IS A DELICIOUS MEAL TO SERVE FOR SUPPER, ACCOMPANIED WITH PLAIN WHITE RICE.

1 kg stewing meat or mutton pieces

250 ml (1 cup) water

2 large onions, finely chopped

5 ml (1 tsp) garlic and ginger paste

12.5 ml (2½ tsp) salt, or to taste

6 black peppercorns

4 whole allspice

60 ml (¼ cup) cooking oil

2 large tomatoes, peeled and grated

60 ml (¼ cup) Worcestershire sauce

30 ml (2 Tbsp) white sugar

500 g frozen peas

500 g frozen baby carrots

5 ml (1 tsp) fine black pepper

6 medium potatoes, peeled and halved

2.5 ml (½ tsp) dried parsley

Wash the meat and drain in a colander. To a large pot on medium heat, add the water and meat, the onions, garlic and ginger paste, salt, peppercorns and allspice. Cook for 15–20 minutes till the meat is tender and the water has cooked away. Add 60 ml (¼ cup) water during cooking if the meat is not yet done. Once all of the water has cooked away, add the oil and simmer for 5 minutes. Add the grated tomatoes, Worcestershire sauce, sugar, frozen veggies and pepper. Simmer for 15–20 minutes till the veggies are tender.

In a separate pot, boil the potatoes in enough water with 5 ml (1 tsp) salt till cooked but still firm. Add the drained potatoes to the stew and stir gently to combine all the ingredients. Simmer, covered, on low heat for 10 minutes. Lastly, sprinkle the parsley over the surface of the stew and simmer for 5 minutes more. Remove from heat and serve with white rice.

TOMATO AND MUSHROOM CHICKEN STEW

SERVES 6

- 1 kg chicken pieces (drumsticks and thighs only)
- 60 ml (¼ cup) cooking oil
- 1 star anise
- 4 whole allspice
- 3 whole cloves
- 6 black peppercorns
- 2 medium onions, finely chopped
- 1 medium green pepper, chopped
- 1 medium fresh green chilli, finely chopped
- 5 ml (1 tsp) garlic and ginger paste
- 30 ml (2 Tbsp) water
- 2 large tomatoes, peeled and grated
- 1 x 415 g tin cream of tomato soup
- 15 ml (1 Tbsp) white sugar
- 10 ml (2 tsp) salt, or to taste
- 2.5 ml (½ tsp) fine black pepper
- 1 ml (¼ tsp) turmeric
- 2.5 ml (½ tsp) cayenne pepper
- 2.5 ml (½ tsp) ground coriander
- 5 ml (1 tsp) mixed dried herbs
- 1 x 250 g punnet button mushrooms, chopped
- 15 ml (1 Tbsp) fresh cream (optional)

Wash, skin and drain the chicken pieces. Set aside in a colander.

Heat the oil in a large pot on medium to high heat and add the star anise, allspice, cloves, and peppercorns. Add the onions, green pepper and chilli and braise till the onions are golden brown. Reduce to medium heat and add the chicken, garlic and ginger paste and water. Simmer for 10 minutes till the chicken is cooked but still firm.

Next, add the grated tomatoes, tomato soup, sugar, salt, pepper, turmeric, cayenne pepper, ground coriander, mixed herbs and mushrooms. Simmer, covered halfway with the lid, for 30–35 minutes on medium to low heat. Remove from heat and drizzle with fresh cream, if using. Serve with white rice and salads.

Rice can be prepared in various ways and can be served with almost any meal. It forms part of a staple diet for both Indians and Malays.

RICE

SWEET YELLOW RICE

SERVES 6

SLIGHTLY SWEET AND FRAGRANT, THIS RICE IS SERVED WITH MANY DISHES. ONE CAN ADD SULTANAS AND FLAKED ALMONDS IF DESIRED.

750 ml (3 cups) long-grain white rice
1.25 litres (5 cups) water
5 ml (1 tsp) turmeric
7.5 ml (1½ tsp) salt
125 g butter or margarine
4 large pieces of stick cinnamon
7 cardamom pods, split open
250 ml (1 cup) white sugar

Wash and drain the rice in a colander. Add the water to a deep pot along with the rice. To this, add the turmeric and salt and boil on medium heat till the rice is half-cooked. The rice grains should still be firm but breakable when crushed between the fingers. Remove from heat and rinse under cold water in a colander. Drain very well.

To a deep pot on medium heat, add the butter, cinnamon and cardamom. As soon as the butter has melted, add the rice along with the sugar. Stir thoroughly, combining all the ingredients. Simmer on low heat for 10–15 minutes, stirring occasionally, till light and fluffy.

MORE THAN SAMOOSAS

BRAISED WHITE RICE

SERVES 6

THIS RICE CAN BE SERVED WITH ALMOST ANY MEAL.

750 ml (3 cups) long-grain white rice
1.25 litres (5 cups) water
15 ml (1 Tbsp) salt
60 ml (¼ cup) butter or margarine
1 whole fresh green chilli, slit midway
3 medium onions, thinly sliced

Wash and drain the rice in a colander. Transfer to a deep pot along with the water. Add the salt and boil on medium heat till half-cooked but still slightly firm. Remove from heat and rinse in a colander. Allow all of the water to drain from the rice and set aside.

To a large frying pan on medium to high heat, add the butter and chilli. Add the onions and braise till golden brown. Transfer the rice to a deep pot and pour the onion mixture over the rice. Cover and simmer on medium to low heat for 10–15 minutes till done. Stir thoroughly. Remove from heat and serve.

Variation: Add 250 ml (1 cup) whole kernel corn to the rice; stir well to combine, and then add the onion mixture.

Savoury rice can be served with most dishes and also makes a light meal or snack on its own.

750 ml (3 cups) long-grain white rice
1.5 litres (6 cups) water
10 ml (2 tsp) salt
2.5 ml (½ tsp) turmeric
250 ml (1 cup) screw noodles
60 ml (¼ cup) ghee or 30 ml (2 Tbsp) butter
2.5 ml (½ tsp) freshly ground black pepper
2 large onions, sliced
1 whole fresh green chilli, slit midway
1 small green pepper, chopped
2.5 ml (½ tsp) red leaf masala
5 ml (1 tsp) Cajun spice
1 x 410 g tin whole kernel corn, drained

SERVES 6

SAVOURY RICE

Wash and drain the rice in a colander. Transfer to a deep pot along with the water, salt and turmeric. Stir and boil on medium heat till the rice grains are half-cooked but still firm. Remove from heat and rinse and drain in a colander. Set aside. Boil the noodles according to packet instructions till al dente. Drain and set aside.

To a large frying pan on medium to high heat, add the ghee or butter. Once hot, add the black pepper, onions, whole chilli and the green pepper and braise till the onions are golden brown. Add the red leaf masala and Cajun spice, stir and simmer on low heat for 2 minutes.

To a large deep pot on medium to low heat, add the rice, noodles, onion mixture and corn. Stir well to combine all the ingredients. Steam for 10 minutes, stirring occasionally. Remove from heat and serve.

KITCHRI RICE

SERVES 6

THIS RICE CAN BE SERVED WITH ALL CURRIES.

125 ml (½ cup) red lentils
750 ml (3 cups) long-grain white rice
1.5 litres (6 cups) water
15 ml (1 Tbsp) salt
125g butter or margarine
3 pieces of stick cinnamon

Presoak the lentils in water for about 1 hour. Rinse the rice in a colander and drain.

To a deep pot on medium to high heat, add the water and salt and bring to a boil. Add the rice and drained lentils and boil for 15–20 minutes till done. Transfer the cooked rice to a colander, rinse under cold water and drain. Set aside.

To a large deep pot on medium heat, add the butter and cinnamon. Once the butter has melted, add the rice and lentil mixture. Stir well, ensuring that all of the rice and butter is mixed. Steam, covered, on low heat for 15 minutes, stirring occasionally. Remove from heat and serve.

FLOP-PROOF WHITE RICE

SERVES 6

THIS IS THE BASIC METHOD FOR PREPARING WHITE RICE.

750 ml (3 cups) long-grain white rice
1.5 litres (6 cups) water
10 ml (2 tsp) salt
10 ml (2 tsp) butter or margarine

Rinse the rice in a colander and drain.

To a large deep pot, add the water, salt and butter. Bring to a boil and add the drained rice. Boil for 10 minutes till half-cooked but still firm. Remove from heat, rinse and drain in a colander.

Transfer the rice to a large ovenproof dish and place in the microwave for 5–6 minutes. Remove from the microwave and serve.

These recipes make great accompaniments to all dishes and are tasty, quick and easy to prepare.

VEGETABLES AND SALADS

This side dish can be served with roasted chicken or meat and is an all-time favourite among children.

1 kg pumpkin, peeled and cut into large cubes
15 ml (1 Tbsp) butter or margarine
3 pieces of stick cinnamon
1 ml (¼ tsp) jeera seeds
1 large onion, finely chopped
15 ml (1 Tbsp) water
2.5 ml (½ tsp) salt
125 ml (½ cup) sugar
1 ml (¼ tsp) chilli powder

SERVES 6

CINNAMON SWEET PUMPKIN

Boil the pumpkin in water till cooked but still firm, and then drain in a colander and set aside.

To a medium pot on medium heat, add the butter, cinnamon, jeera seeds and onion. Braise till golden brown, then add the water and cook till the onion is soft. Next, add the salt, sugar and chilli powder. Stir and add the pumpkin pieces. Stir gently, cover and steam on low heat for 10 minutes. Remove from heat and serve.

GLAZED CARROTS

SERVES 6

SERVE WITH ROASTS, BOTH CHICKEN AND MEAT.

6 large carrots, scraped, cut into 3 and halved
4 pieces of stick cinnamon
5 ml (1 tsp) butter or margarine
2.5 ml (½ tsp) salt
300 ml (1 ¼ cups) water

Place all the ingredients in a pot on medium to high heat and bring to the boil. Simmer till the carrots are cooked but still firm. Remove from heat, drain and transfer to a serving dish. Dot with extra butter while still hot.

GREEN BEAN BAJIE

SERVES 6

SERVE WITH MINCE KEBABS, SWEET YELLOW RICE OR FRIED POTATO WEDGES.

60 ml (¼ cup) cooking oil
1 large onion, chopped
6 black peppercorns
4 whole allspice
1 large tomato, peeled and grated
60 ml (¼ cup) water
5 ml (1 tsp) garlic and ginger paste
2.5 ml (½ tsp) salt, or to taste
15 ml (1 Tbsp) white sugar
15 ml (1 Tbsp) Worcestershire sauce
2.5 ml (½ tsp) ground jeera
2.5 ml (½ tsp) red leaf masala
1 ml (¼ tsp) chilli powder
2 x 410 g tins green beans, drained

To a medium-sized pot on medium to high heat, add the cooking oil and heat. To this, add the onion, peppercorns and allspice. Braise till the onion is golden brown. Add the grated tomato along with the water, garlic and ginger paste, salt and sugar. Cook on medium heat for 5 minutes. Add the Worcestershire sauce, ground jeera, red leaf masala and chilli powder. Simmer for 5 minutes more on medium to low heat. Lastly, add the green beans and simmer on low heat for 10–15 minutes till done. Remove from heat and serve as described above.

VEGETABLES AND SALADS

CAULIFLOWER AND BROCCOLI BAKE

SERVES 6

THIS DISH MAKES A GREAT ACCOMPANIMENT TO ALMOST ANY ROASTED MEAT.

1 medium head cauliflower, broken into florets
1 medium head broccoli, broken into florets
500 ml (2 cups) water
12.5 ml (2½ tsp) salt
30 ml (2 Tbsp) butter or margarine
1 medium onion, finely chopped
5 ml (1 tsp) freshly ground black pepper
1 ml (¼ tsp) cayenne pepper
2.5 ml (½ tsp) Cajun spice
2.5 ml (½ tsp) mother-in-law masala
15 ml (1 Tbsp) white sugar
500 ml (2 cups) fresh cream
500 ml (2 cups) grated sweetmilk (Gouda) cheese
5 ml (1 tsp) mixed dried herbs

Preheat the oven to 180 °C. Rinse the cauliflower and broccoli in a colander and drain. Place the cauliflower and broccoli in a large pot along with the water and 10 ml (2 tsp) of the salt, and bring to the boil. Boil till cooked but still slightly firm. Drain and set aside.

To a saucepan on medium heat, add the butter and heat. To this, add the onion and black pepper and braise till the onion is golden. Add the cayenne pepper, Cajun spice, remaining salt, mother-in-law masala and sugar. Stir and simmer on low heat for 2 minutes. Add the cream, stir and simmer for 5 minutes. Add 250 ml (1 cup) of the grated cheese and stir till all of the cheese has melted and a smooth consistency is reached. Place the cauliflower and broccoli florets in an ovenproof dish, pour the sauce over the top, and sprinkle with the remaining cheese and mixed herbs. Bake till the cheese melts and turns golden in colour. Remove from oven and serve.

STEWED SWEET POTATO

SERVES 4–6

THIS DISH CAN BE SERVED AS A SIDE DISH, OR AS A DESSERT, WITH WARM CUSTARD AND A DASH OF WHIPPED CREAM.

4 large sweet potatoes, peeled, washed and cut into rounds
125 ml (½ cup) water
4 pieces of stick cinnamon
5 cardamom pods, split open
10 ml (2 tsp) rose water
2.5 ml (½ tsp) vanilla essence
10 ml (2 tsp) butter or margarine
A pinch of salt
200 ml (¾ cup) sugar

Place the sweet potatoes in a large saucepan along with the water, cinnamon, cardamom, rose water, vanilla essence, butter and salt. Bring to the boil and then add the sugar. Cook on medium heat till the water becomes syrupy and the sweet potatoes are tender and soft. Serve hot as described above.

PERI-PERI POTATO WEDGES

SERVES 6

THESE POTATO WEDGES CAN BE SERVED WITH ALMOST ANY MEAL AND THEY MAKE A GREAT SNACK ON THEIR OWN WITH A DIP.

6 medium potatoes, peeled and cut into wedges
Cake flour for coating
Enough oil for deep-frying
A sprinkle of peri-peri powder, depending on taste preference

Place the washed and drained potato wedges in a plastic microwaveable bowl. Heat for about 4–5 minutes. Remove and dip each wedge into the flour, coating the entire wedge. Immediately fry in hot oil till lightly golden. Remove and place on paper towel to drain off excess oil. Place on a serving platter and sprinkle with peri-peri powder.

BAKED BEAN SALAD

SERVES 6

THIS COLD SALAD IS USUALLY SERVED WITH A BARBECUE, BUT IT ALSO MAKES A GREAT ACCOMPANIMENT TO CRUMBED CHICKEN.

1 x 410 g tin baked beans in tomato sauce
1 x 410 g tin cream-style sweetcorn
1 medium onion, finely chopped
1 small green pepper, chopped
1 medium fresh green chilli, finely chopped
1 ml (¼ tsp) salt, or to taste
2.5 ml (½ tsp) freshly ground black pepper
1 ml (¼ tsp) cayenne pepper (optional)

Place all of the ingredients in a large bowl and mix well, ensuring all ingredients are thoroughly combined. Refrigerate till ready to serve.

Variation: If preferred, braise the onion and green pepper in 15 ml (1 Tbsp) butter till golden brown, and then add to the remaining ingredients.

This salad is usually served with curries, breyanis and akhnis.

4 large tomatoes
1 large onion
15 ml (1 Tbsp) salt
1 small fresh green chilli, finely chopped
60 ml (¼ cup) chopped fresh dhania
60 ml (¼ cup) brown vinegar
15 ml (1 Tbsp) sugar, or to taste

SERVES 4

TOMATO AND ONION SALAD

Chop the tomatoes into tiny cubes, removing most of the pulp and seeds. (You can also use halved Roma tomatoes.) Transfer to a serving bowl.

Chop the onion and transfer to a colander. Add the salt and squeeze the onions, removing most of the juice. Rinse in cold water and drain.

Add the onion and remaining ingredients to the tomatoes and mix well. Store in the refrigerator. Serve as described above.

TUNA SALAD

SERVES 6

THIS SALAD CAN BE EATEN ON ROLLS, SANDWICHES OR WITH ANY OF YOUR FAVOURITE BREADS.

1 large onion, finely chopped
15 ml (1 Tbsp) salt
2 x 185 g tins tuna, drained
1 medium tomato
1 small fresh green chilli, finely chopped
4 lettuce leaves, shredded
2.5 ml (½ tsp) freshly ground black pepper
1 ml (¼ tsp) cayenne pepper
30–45 ml (2–3 Tbsp) mayonnaise
Cocktail tomatoes and dried mixed herbs for garnishing

Place the chopped onion in a colander. Add the salt and squeeze the onions, removing most of the juice. Rinse and drain.

Combine the onion with the remaining ingredients and an extra pinch of salt and mix well. Garnish with halved cocktail tomatoes and a sprinkle of dried mixed herbs.

EGG SALAD

SERVES 4–6

THIS SALAD IS A FAVOURITE SERVED WITH BREADS AND CAN ALSO BE USED AS A DIP FOR CRISPS.

6 large hard-boiled eggs
1 large onion, finely chopped
15 ml (1 Tbsp) salt
1 small fresh green chilli, finely chopped
1 ml (¼ tsp) cayenne pepper
2.5 ml (½ tsp) freshly ground black pepper
A pinch of salt
A pinch of dried mixed herbs
30 ml (2 Tbsp) mayonnaise

Cut the eggs into quarters and mash roughly (or cut them into halves for a chunkier salad). Set aside.

Place the onion in a colander with the salt and squeeze out the excess juice. Rinse in cold water and drain.

Combine all of the ingredients, add an extra pinch of salt and mix well. Serve as photographed or as described above.

VEGETABLES AND SALADS

The key to perfectly baked bread is in the kneading of the dough. Dough is sufficiently kneaded when it springs back into shape after being pressed lightly with a finger.

BREADS AND PASTRY

NAAN BREAD ROLLS

MAKES ABOUT 24

THESE ROLLS CAN BE SERVED WITH BASICALLY ANYTHING, SUCH AS SOUPS, EGG OR TUNA SALADS, OR ON THEIR OWN WITH PRESERVES AND CHEESE.

2 large potatoes, peeled
30 ml (2 Tbsp) butter or margarine
625 ml (2½ cups) warm full-cream milk
4 x 250 ml (4 cups) cake flour
20 g (2 sachets) instant dry yeast
15 ml (1 Tbsp) white sugar
5 ml (1 tsp) salt
2 large eggs, beaten
1 extra beaten egg to glaze tops of rolls
Poppy seeds for sprinkling (optional)

Boil the potatoes in salted water till soft. Drain, add the butter and mash. Add 125 ml (½ cup) of the milk and mix till smooth. Sift the flour into a large mixing bowl. Add the yeast, sugar and salt and stir, mixing well. Make a well in the centre of the flour mixture and add the 2 beaten eggs, the mashed potatoes and the remaining milk. Mix to form a soft dough, adding extra flour if required. Knead till the dough is soft and elastic. Press the dough lightly with a finger; if the dough springs back, it is sufficiently kneaded. Sprinkle the dough with flour, cover with a cloth and leave in a warm place for 1 hour, till doubled in size. Preheat the oven to 180 °C.

Transfer the dough to a floured surface and knead lightly. Divide into 24 equal pieces and roll into balls. Lightly grease a baking sheet with a little cooking oil. Place the balls on the baking sheet, packed closely together and flattened slightly, so that the balls take on a squashed shape. Brush with beaten egg and sprinkle over the poppy seeds. Leave to stand for 15 minutes, away from drafts, before baking for 30 minutes, or till lightly golden brown. Remove from oven. Naan rolls can be served hot, straight from the oven, with cheese and preserves. Alternatively, cool first and then store in an airtight container till needed.

PURI

SERVES 6-8

THIS IS AN INDIAN PUFFED BREAD, WHICH IS VERY LIGHT AND IS USUALLY SERVED WITH CURRIES.

750 ml (3 cups) cake flour
15 ml (1 Tbsp) baking powder
A pinch of salt
40 ml (8 tsp) butter or margarine
1 large egg, beaten
250 ml (1 cup) warm full-cream milk
Sufficient oil for deep-frying

Sift the flour and baking powder into a large mixing bowl. Add the salt and the butter and rub together till the mixture resembles fine breadcrumbs.

Add the beaten egg together with the warm milk, and mix to form a soft dough. If the dough becomes too sticky, add a little extra flour and knead lightly. This dough does not have to be kneaded much, as it does not need to rise.

Transfer the dough to a floured surface and roll out into a large square that is 5 mm thick. Cut into even squares measuring about 6 cm x 6 cm.

Deep-fry in hot oil for 2 minutes, or till puffed up and lightly golden. Drain on paper towel and serve.

BREADS AND PASTRY

ROTI

4 x 250 ml (4 cups) cake flour
5 ml (1 tsp) baking powder
5 ml (1 tsp) salt
60 ml (¼ cup) butter or margarine
200 ml (¾ cup) warm water
250 ml (1 cup) ghee

MAKES 10

Roti is a flat, flaky Indian bread, which is often served with curries.

Sift the flour and baking powder into a large mixing bowl. Add the salt and butter and rub together till the mixture resembles fine breadcrumbs. Add the warm water, little by little, and mix till a smooth dough is formed. Transfer the dough to a floured surface and divide into 10 equal portions. Roll each portion between your palms into a round ball.

Working with two portions at a time, place two balls on a floured surface and roll out using a rolling pin till they are the size of a large plate and about 5 mm thick. Spread each round with 10 ml (2 tsp) ghee and sprinkle with flour. Make a vertical slit of about 4 cm at the bottom of each round, and roll upwards away from you, forming a long sausage. Take the long piece of dough, hold down one end on the table with an index finger, and roll the rest up the length of your index finger, remove your finger and place the remaining end in the centre, pressing the tower of dough down firmly, forming a ball. Roll each ball into a large round of about 5 mm thick.

Place a large shallow pot on medium to high heat, add 15 ml (1 Tbsp) ghee, reduce heat to medium and add the raw roti. Fry on both sides for 2 minutes, or till golden in colour. Add more ghee for each roti. Place the hot roti in a dishcloth and slap together between your palms. Lay flat on paper towel and serve warm.

Note: As a substitute for ghee, place 125 ml (½ cup) oil with 250 g butter in a pot and melt on medium heat. Allow to cool and pour into a jar with a tight-fitting lid. This may be stored at room temperature for up to a month.

5 x 250 ml (5 cups) cake flour
10 ml (2 tsp) salt
30 g (3 sachets) instant dry yeast
15 ml (1 Tbsp) white sugar
5 ml (1 tsp) anise seeds
2 large potatoes, peeled
60 ml (¼ cup) butter or margarine
125 ml (½ cup) warm full-cream milk
3 large eggs, beaten
1 large egg, beaten, to glaze tops of rolls
Sesame and poppy seeds for sprinkling

MAKES 20

These rolls can be served with any meal or even just with preserves and cheese.

KITKE ROLLS

Sift the flour and salt into a large mixing bowl. Add the yeast, sugar and anise seeds. Stir to mix. Boil the potatoes in salted water till soft. Drain and mash in a separate bowl. Add the butter and mash till fine. Add 125 ml (½ cup) of the warm milk and stir till smooth and creamy.

Make a well in the centre of the flour mixture and add the 3 eggs and the mashed potato. Mix together to form a soft dough. Add more flour if the dough is too wet, or more warm milk if the dough is too dry.

Sprinkle the dough with flour, cover with a dishcloth and leave in a warm place to rise for 1 hour, or till doubled in size. Preheat the oven to 180 °C.

Knock down the dough and transfer to a floured surface. Divide into 20 equal portions and roll each portion into rounds. Place on a greased baking tray. Brush with the beaten egg and sprinkle half with sesame seeds and half with poppy seeds. Leave to stand for 15 minutes. Bake in the preheated oven for 30 minutes, or till golden.

Variation: These rolls can be plaited or knotted for a different effect.

BREAD

750 ml (3 cups) cake flour
5 ml (1 tsp) salt
10 ml (2 tsp) sugar
20 g (2 sachets) instant dry yeast
375 ml (1½ cups) warm full-cream milk
1 large egg, beaten

TOPPING

60 ml (¼ cup) cooking oil
1 large onion, thinly sliced
1 fresh green chilli, finely chopped
8 cocktail tomatoes, halved
2.5 ml (½ tsp) salt
5 ml (1 tsp) crushed garlic
5 olives, pitted and sliced

MAKES 2 BREADS

Focaccia is a flat bread of Italian origin and can be enjoyed on its own or with grated cheese. This is my mother's original recipe.

FOCACCIA

Sift the flour and salt into a large mixing bowl. Add 5 ml (1 tsp) sugar and stir.

In a separate bowl, mix the yeast with 125 ml (½ cup) of the warm milk and the remaining sugar, and leave in a warm place to froth for 8–10 minutes. Add the egg and the yeast mixture to the flour. Mix to a soft dough by adding the rest of the warm milk. Sprinkle the dough with a little flour, cover with a dishcloth and leave in a warm place to rise for 1 hour, or till doubled in size. Preheat the oven to 180 °C.

To a frying pan on medium heat, add the oil, onion and chilli and braise till golden. Add the tomatoes, salt and garlic and cook for 2 minutes. Remove from heat, set aside and allow to cool.

Place the dough on a floured surface and divide into two equal portions. Shape the dough into oblong, flattish loaves and place on a greased baking sheet.

Spoon the onion mixture onto the loaves and spread evenly across the top. Sprinkle the olive slices over the top and set aside for 15 minutes. Bake in the preheated oven for 35–40 minutes, or till done. Remove from oven and cool slightly before slicing.

This section covers delicious dessert recipes, both warm and cold. Some are really quick and easy to prepare and are ideal for when your time is limited.

PUDDINGS, TARTS AND FRITTERS

POTATO PUDDING
WITH STEWED FRUIT

SERVES 8

4 large potatoes, peeled
125 g butter or margarine
6 large eggs, beaten till thick and frothy
250 ml (1 cup) sugar
1 litre (4 cups) full-cream milk
20 ml (4 tsp) vanilla essence
5 ml (1 tsp) almond essence
60 ml (¼ cup) cake flour
6 cardamom pods, split open
5 pieces of stick cinnamon
2.5 ml (½ tsp) grated nutmeg for sprinkling

Preheat the oven to 180 °C. Boil the potatoes in salted water till completely soft. Drain in a colander and transfer to a large mixing bowl. Add the butter and mash together with the potatoes. Stir to form a smooth and creamy consistency. Add the eggs and sugar and beat till creamy and thick. Add the milk, little by little, beating well after each addition. Add the vanilla and almond essence and beat well. Sift in the flour and beat well till the mixture becomes thick and creamy. Add the cardamom and cinnamon and stir.

Grease a large ovenproof dish (approx. 37 cm x 27 cm x 5 cm deep) with butter and pour in the pudding batter. Sprinkle with nutmeg and bake in the preheated oven for 1 hour, or till done. Leave to stand for 10 minutes before serving with the warm stewed fruit.

STEWED FRUIT

500 g mixed dried fruit
375 ml (1½ cups) water
3 pieces of stick cinnamon
250 ml (1 cup) sugar
5 ml (1 tsp) butter or margarine

Add all the ingredients to a saucepan on medium heat and cook for 15–20 minutes, till the water becomes a thick syrup and the fruits are tender.

This delicious chilled dessert is a favourite among the Malays and is always served on Eid Day.

2 x 85 g packets of jelly (1 red and 1 green)
1 x ready-made sponge loaf
1 x 420 g tin sliced peaches, drained
250 ml (1 cup) fresh cream
10 ml (2 tsp) castor sugar
1 litre (4 cups) ready-made custard
250 ml (1 cup) pecan nuts, chopped
1 Flake chocolate

SERVES 10

TRIFLE

The day before, prepare the jellies in separate bowls according to packet instructions – the jelly must be firmly set. Slice the sponge cake and arrange the slices along the sides and bottom of a large glass serving bowl (about 30 cm in diameter and 15–20 cm deep). Spread the peaches over the layer of sponge.

Beat the fresh cream with the castor sugar till slightly past soft peak stage. Refrigerate for 15 minutes. Spread half of the custard over the peaches. Scoop all of the green jelly over the custard layer. Spread half of the cream over the green jelly. Directly over this, sprinkle all of the chopped pecan nuts. Spread all of the red jelly over the nuts, then the remaining custard over the red jelly layer. Lastly, use a fork to spread the remaining cream evenly over the top. Sprinkle with crushed Flake and refrigerate for at least 5 hours before serving.

VERMICELLI (LOCKSHEN)

SERVES 8–10

- 125 g butter or margarine
- 3 pieces of stick cinnamon
- 3 cardamom pods, split open
- 500 g extra-fine vermicelli (lockshen)
- 625 ml (2½ cups) water
- 5 ml (1 tsp) vanilla essence
- 10 ml (2 tsp) rose water
- 250 ml (1 cup) sugar

This is a tasty warm dessert that can be enjoyed anytime. It is a favourite during the holy month of Ramadan.

To a large pot on medium to high heat, add the butter and heat. Add the cinnamon, cardamom and vermicelli, reduce to medium heat and braise till the vermicelli is golden brown. Add the water, vanilla essence, rose water and sugar. Stir well and simmer on low heat for 15–20 minutes, stirring frequently and ensuring that the vermicelli does not become too dry. If this occurs, just add a dash of boiling water and simmer for 5 minutes longer. The vermicelli should be soft, tender and moist. Serve hot.

Variation: If preferred, add 125 ml (½ cup) seedless raisons to the vermicelli, just before adding the water, and cook in exactly the same manner.

LOCKSHEN DELIGHT

- 500 ml (2 cups) water
- 250 g extra-fine vermicelli (lockshen)
- 4 large eggs
- 300 ml (1¼ cups) white sugar
- 10 ml (2 tsp) almond essence
- 2 x 250 g tubs smooth cottage cheese
- 60 ml (¼ cup) butter or margarine
- 125 ml (½ cup) pecan nuts, chopped
- 125 ml (½ cup) castor sugar
- 60 ml (¼ cup) ground cinnamon

Preheat the oven to 180 °C. Place the water in a large pot on medium to high heat and bring to the boil. Add the vermicelli and boil till soft and tender. Drain and set aside.

Beat the eggs in a separate mixing bowl. Add the sugar and beat till thick and creamy. Add the almond essence and cottage cheese and beat well. Grease a large ovenproof dish (35 cm x 25 cm x 5 cm deep) with the butter. Spread the cooked vermicelli over the bottom of the dish and spread the cottage cheese mixture evenly over the vermicelli. Scatter the pecan nuts over the cottage cheese. Mix the castor sugar and cinnamon together and sprinkle over the top, making sure to cover the entire pudding. Bake for 45–55 minutes, or till done and golden brown. Switch off the oven and leave the pudding in the oven for 10 minutes. Remove and leave to stand for 10 minutes more before serving.

PUDDINGS, TARTS AND FRITTERS

BREAD PUDDING

SERVES 8

BREAD PUDDING IS A DELICIOUSLY SATISFYING ANYTIME TREAT. SERVE WITH A DRIZZLE OF HONEY OR GOLDEN SYRUP.

8 slices of stale white bread

1 litre (4 cups) full-cream milk

6 large eggs

250 ml (1 cup) sugar

15 ml (1 Tbsp) cornflour

10 ml (2 tsp) vanilla essence

15 ml (1 Tbsp) apricot jam, melted

4 pieces of stick cinnamon

6 cardamom pods, split open

15 ml (1 Tbsp) castor sugar

2.5 ml (½ tsp) ground cinnamon

60 ml (¼ cup) flaked almonds

Preheat the oven to 180 °C. Soak the bread slices in 750 ml (3 cups) of the milk for 10–15 minutes. Mash well and set aside.

Beat the eggs in a large mixing bowl till light and frothy. Add the sugar and beat till thick and creamy. Add the bread mixture and mix. In a separate bowl, mix the remaining milk with the cornflour till smooth. Add this to the bread mixture along with the vanilla essence and jam and beat well, combining all of the ingredients. Add the stick cinnamon and cardamom and stir. Grease a large ovenproof dish (25 cm x 25 cm x 4–5 cm deep) with butter. Pour the batter into the dish. Mix the castor sugar and ground cinnamon together and sprinkle over the top of the pudding, along with the flaked almonds. Bake in the preheated oven for 45–60 minutes, till golden brown in colour. Remove from the oven and leave to stand for 10 minutes before serving.

SAGO PUDDING

SERVES 8–10

THIS TASTY PUDDING IS BEST ENJOYED WITH A DOLLOP OF HONEY.

250 g sago, soaked in water for 1 hour
1 litre (4 cups) full-cream milk
6 large eggs
10 ml (2 tsp) vanilla essence
2.5 ml (½ tsp) almond essence
A pinch of salt
300 ml (1¼ cups) sugar
15 ml (1 Tbsp) cornflour mixed with
125 ml (½ cup) full-cream milk
20 ml (4 tsp) butter or margarine
4 pieces of stick cinnamon
6 cardamom pods, split open
15 ml (1 Tbsp) castor sugar
2.5 ml (½ tsp) ground cinnamon

Preheat the oven to 180 °C. Drain the sago and place in a saucepan along with 500 ml (2 cups) of the milk and boil till soft and transparent. Allow to cool and set aside.

Add the eggs to a large mixing bowl and beat till light and frothy. Add the remaining milk and mix. Add the pre-cooked sago and mix thoroughly. Add the vanilla essence, almond essence, salt and sugar and beat well. Mix in the dissolved cornflour.

Grease a large ovenproof dish (25 cm x 25 cm x 4–5 cm deep) with butter. Pour the batter into the dish and spread evenly with a spatula. Drop the 20 ml (4 tsp) of butter randomly into the pudding, and do the same with the stick cinnamon and cardamom. Sprinkle with a mixture of the castor sugar and ground cinnamon.

Bake in the preheated oven for 50 minutes, or till done and golden brown in colour. Switch off the oven and leave the pudding in the oven for 10 minutes with the door open. Remove from oven and leave to stand for another 10 minutes before serving.

MILK TART

SERVES 8-10

MILK TART IS ALWAYS SERVED AT MALAY FUNCTIONS OR PARTIES.

CRUST

125 g soft butter or margarine

125 ml (½ cup) sugar

1 large egg

60 ml (¼ cup) cooking oil

750 ml (3 cups) cake flour

FILLING

8 large eggs

1 litre (4 cups) full-cream milk

250 ml (1 cup) sugar

30 ml (2 Tbsp) vanilla essence

60 ml (¼ cup) custard powder

½ x 397g tin condensed milk

30 ml (2 Tbsp) cake flour

6 cardamom pods, split open

6 pieces of stick cinnamon

Grated nutmeg for sprinkling

Preheat the oven to 180 °C.

To make the crust: Place the butter and sugar in a mixing bowl and cream together. Add the egg and whisk till thick and creamy. Add the oil and mix. Sift in the flour gradually and mix to form a soft biscuit-like dough. Grease a heavy-based rectangular ovenproof dish (37 cm x 27 cm) lightly with butter and line with the dough mixture, along the bottom and sides of the dish.

To make the filling: Whisk the eggs till light and frothy. Add the milk and beat well. Add the sugar and vanilla essence and mix. Sift the custard powder into the milk mixture and beat well, making sure there are no lumps. Add the condensed milk and mix well. Sift the cake flour into the mixture and beat thoroughly till a creamy consistency is formed.

Pour the filling into the crust and scatter the cardamom pods and stick cinnamon on top. Sprinkle lightly with nutmeg and bake for 1 hour. Switch off the oven, open the door and leave to cool for 10 minutes. Remove from oven and leave to stand for 10 minutes more before serving.

COCONUT TARTLETS

MAKES 12

COCONUT TARTLETS ARE A DELICIOUS SWEET TREAT TO SERVE AT TEA TIME, AND ARE ALWAYS SERVED ON EID DAY.

1 x 400–500 g portion puff pastry
1 large egg, beaten
Icing sugar for dusting

FILLING
375 ml (1½ cups) desiccated coconut
4 cardamom pods, split open
4 pieces of stick cinnamon
15 ml (1 Tbsp) butter or margarine
250 ml (1 cup) sugar
200 ml (¾ cup) water

To make the filling: To a small saucepan on medium heat, add all of the filling ingredients, and boil till all of the water has cooked away but the mixture is still moist and has formed a light syrup. Set aside and leave to cool.

Preheat the oven to 220 °C. Use the puff pastry to line a 12-hole tartlet tray. On a floured surface, roll out the pastry to 7 mm thick and cut with a round cutter. Place the pastry rounds in the tart moulds and fill with the coconut filling. Use strips or stars of pastry to cover the tops of the tarts, sealing the edges of the casings. Brush the pastry with the beaten egg and bake for 30 minutes, or till golden. Dust with icing sugar while still hot. Turn out the tarts from the tray and cool.

Variation: To make jam-and-coconut tarts, add 5 ml (1 tsp) apricot jam to the tart casings before adding the coconut filling. For plain jam tarts, omit the coconut filling and fill the casings with jam, any flavour of choice.

This tart is best served warm with whipped fresh cream. It can be reheated in the microwave.

FILLING

1 x 420 g tin pie apple slices

250 ml (1 cup) sugar

15 ml (1 Tbsp) ground cinnamon

2.5 ml (½ tsp) ground mixed spice

2.5 ml (½ tsp) ground ginger

CRUST

125 g soft butter or margarine

250 ml (1 cup) sugar

1 large egg

60 ml (¼ cup) cooking oil

5 ml (1 tsp) vanilla essence

875 ml (3½ cups) cake flour

SERVES 6–8

APPLE CRUMBLE

Preheat the oven to 180 °C.

To make the filling: Place all the filling ingredients in a saucepan on medium heat. Cook on medium to low heat till a thick syrup has formed. Remove from heat and allow to cool.

To make the crust: Place the butter in a mixing bowl and cream together with the sugar till thick and creamy. Add the egg, cooking oil and vanilla essence, and beat till thick and creamy. Gradually sift in the flour and mix to form a soft dough.

To assemble and bake: Grease a standard size pie tin lightly with butter. Line the bottom and sides of the dish with half of the dough. Drain some of the juice from the apple filling, but not all of it. Fill the pie casing with the apple mixture. Coarsely grate the remaining dough all over the top of the apples. Bake in the preheated oven for 45 minutes till done and lightly golden. Remove from oven and leave to cool slightly before slicing. Serve as described above, or with vanilla ice cream.

POTATO FRITTERS

MAKES 24

THIS MAKES A GREAT SNACK SERVED AT ANY TIME, AND IS ALWAYS A FAVOURITE DURING THE MONTH OF RAMADAN.

5 large potatoes, peeled and cubed
A pinch of salt
1 large egg, beaten
5 ml (1 tsp) almond essence
2.5 ml (½ tsp) ground cinnamon
1 ml (¼ tsp) grated nutmeg
15 ml (1 Tbsp) sugar
500 ml (2 cups) cake flour
5 ml (1 tsp) baking powder
250 ml (1 cup) full-cream milk
Cooking oil for frying
Castor sugar and ground cinnamon
   for sprinkling

Boil the potatoes in water with the pinch of salt till completely soft. Place the drained potatoes in a bowl and mash till fine. Stir till the mash becomes smooth. Add the egg, almond essence, cinnamon, nutmeg and sugar and mix well. Sift in the cake flour and baking powder. Add milk gradually while mixing to form a smooth batter. Add more milk if the mixture is too thick; the batter should not be too runny either.

In a large pan on high heat, heat enough oil for shallow frying. Once the oil sizzles, reduce heat to medium and drop tablespoonsful of mixture into the oil. Fry for about 2 minutes on one side, or till the top of the fritter bubbles, then turn and fry the other side till lightly golden brown. Remove and drain on paper towel. Arrange on a serving platter and sprinkle with a mixture of castor sugar and ground cinnamon.

PUMPKIN FRITTERS

MAKES 24

PUMPKIN FRITTERS HAVE ALWAYS BEEN A FAVOURITE OF MINE. MY MOTHER WOULD MAKE THEM ON COLD WINTER EVENINGS AND SERVE THEM WITH HOT BEVERAGES.

400 g pumpkin, peeled and cubed
1 large egg, beaten
375 ml (1½ cups) cake flour
5 ml (1 tsp) baking powder
1 ml (¼ tsp) grated nutmeg
2.5 ml (½ tsp) ground cinnamon
A pinch of salt
A pinch of castor sugar (optional)
10 ml (2 tsp) butter, melted
125 ml (½ cup) full-cream milk
Cooking oil for frying
Castor sugar and ground cinnamon for sprinkling

In a medium-size pot on medium to high heat, boil the pumpkin till cooked and soft. Drain, transfer to a large mixing bowl and mash the pumpkin. Add the rest of the ingredients and mix to form a smooth, slightly thick batter. Add more milk if the batter is too thick.

Heat a frying pan with shallow oil on medium heat. Drop tablespoonsful of mixture into the hot oil and fry on both sides till golden. Remove and drain on paper towel. Arrange on a serving platter and dust with cinnamon-sugar.

Variation: For banana fritters, substitute the pumpkin with 5 large, mashed bananas. Follow the recipe in exactly the same manner.

These scrumptious recipes are great for any occasion and are easy to prepare.

CAKES AND BISCUITS

These light, decadent puffs are great to serve at parties and are very versatile, as the variety of fillings is endless.

250 ml (1 cup) water
250 g butter
250 ml (1 cup) cake flour
3 large eggs

MAKES ABOUT 24

ÉCLAIRS

Preheat the oven to 180 °C.

Place the water in a small saucepan and bring to the boil. Immediately add the butter and allow to melt in the water. Remove from heat and add all the sifted flour. Mix with a wooden spoon till the mixture forms a ball in the centre of the saucepan. Transfer the dough to a mixing bowl and allow to cool for about 10 minutes. Once cool, add the eggs, one by one, beating well after each addition till a stiff batter is formed.

Grease a large baking sheet with cooking oil and drop teaspoonsful of the mixture onto the baking sheet, allowing room for spreading. Bake in the preheated oven for 45 minutes. Switch off the oven and leave the éclairs in the oven, with the door open, to dry out and cool off. Slit open and fill as desired.

CHOCOLATE ÉCLAIRS

1 x 250 g slab plain milk chocolate
2 x 170 g tins Nestlé dessert cream
500 ml (2 cups) fresh cream, whipped
Fresh mint leaves and icing sugar for decorating

Melt the chocolate in the microwave for 1–2 minutes, checking and stirring every 30 seconds, till completely melted. Add the dessert cream and mix till smooth and shiny. Fill the éclairs with whipped fresh cream and coat the top half of the éclairs with chocolate. Place on a serving platter and decorate with a few mint leaves and a dusting of icing sugar.

STRAWBERRY CREAM ÉCLAIRS

300–350 g strawberries, hulled and chopped
60 ml (¼ cup) sugar
500 ml (2 cups) fresh cream, whipped
Fresh mint leaves and icing sugar for decorating

Place the chopped strawberries in a mixing bowl. Add the sugar and mix well. Leave to stand in the refrigerator for 10 minutes before using. Fill the éclairs with whipped cream, then the strawberries and dust the tops liberally with icing sugar.

Variation: For banana éclairs, fill the éclairs with mashed banana before adding the whipped cream, and coat the tops with a drizzle of melted chocolate.

CAKES AND BISCUITS

VANILLA SWISS ROLL

SPONGE
3 large eggs
200 ml (¾ cup) castor sugar
10 ml (2 tsp) vanilla essence
250 ml (1 cup) self-raising flour
10 ml (2 tsp) baking powder
1 ml (¼ tsp) bicarbonate of soda

MAKES 1 CAKE

To make the sponge: Preheat the oven to 220 °C. Beat the eggs till light and frothy. Add the castor sugar and beat together till thick and creamy. Add the vanilla essence and mix. Sift in the flour, baking powder and bicarbonate of soda. Mix till smooth. Grease a swiss roll tin (35 cm x 25 cm x 1.5 cm deep), including the sides and corners. Pour the batter into the tin and spread evenly with a spatula. Bake in the preheated oven for 12–15 minutes, or till the sides of the cake pull away from the tin. Before removing the cake from the oven, dampen a clean kitchen cloth and lay it out on a flat, even surface. Remove the cake and immediately flip it out onto the damp cloth. Allow to cool.

FILLING
1 x 395 g tin caramel, stirred till smooth
250 ml (1 cup) fresh cream, whipped with a pinch of castor sugar

To assemble: Once the cake has cooled completely, spread with a layer of caramel and then a layer of whipped cream. Roll up carefully using the damp cloth. Carefully transfer the cake to a piece of wax paper, large enough to accommodate the size of the cake, and dust liberally with icing sugar. Cut off both ends of the cake and discard. Pull the bottom and top edges of the wax paper towards the cake and twist the edges, sealing the cake. Refrigerate for 10 minutes before serving.

Variations: Replace the caramel with 300–350 g of washed, drained and chopped strawberries, mixed with 60 ml (¼ cup) sugar. Leave this mixture to stand in the refrigerator for 10 minutes before using.

To make a chocolate swiss roll, replace the 250 ml (1 cup) of self-raising flour with 200 ml (¾ cup) of self-raising flour and add 60 ml (¼ cup) cocoa powder. For the filling, use 1 x 250 g slab plain milk chocolate, melted, and mix it with 2 x 170 g tins Nestlé dessert cream till smooth and shiny. Spread the sponge with the melted chocolate mixture and top with a layer of whipped cream. Roll up and dust liberally with icing sugar.

CHOCOLATE SPONGE

4 large eggs
375 ml (1½ cups) sugar
5 ml (1 tsp) vanilla essence
125 ml (½ cup) cooking oil
125 ml (½ cup) cocoa powder
250 ml (1 cup) boiling water
500 ml (2 cups) self-raising flour
5 ml (1 tsp) baking powder

SERVES 10–12

This chocolate cake recipe is really very easy and won't let you down.

NEVER-FAIL CHOCOLATE CAKE

Preheat the oven to 190 °C.

Beat the eggs till light and frothy. Add the sugar and beat till thick and creamy. Add the vanilla essence and oil and beat well. Mix the cocoa with the boiling water till smooth, and then cool. Once cooled, add the cocoa mixture to the egg mixture and mix well. Lastly, sift in the flour and baking powder and mix till smooth. Grease a rectangular baking tin (37 cm x 27 cm x 5 cm deep) with butter, pour in the batter and spread evenly with a spatula. Bake for 20 minutes, or till the cake edges start to pull away from the tin. Test with a skewer if uncertain; if the skewer comes out clean, the cake is done. Turn out onto a wire rack. Once cooled, transfer to a serving tray or dish before decorating.

TOPPING

1 x 250 g slab plain milk chocolate, melted
2 x 170 g tins Nestlé dessert cream
Whipped cream for piping (optional)
Sliced strawberries for decorating

Mix the melted chocolate with the dessert cream till smooth and shiny. Once the cake has cooled completely, spread a thick layer of chocolate on the top and sides of the cake. If desired, pipe whipped cream rosettes along the edge of the cake and in the centre, and decorate with sliced strawberries.

CAKES AND BISCUITS

BANANA LOAF CAKE

MAKES 1 LOAF

THIS EASY LOAF CAKE IS GREAT TO SERVE ANY TIME, AND IS REALLY DELICIOUS SPREAD WITH BUTTER.

2 large eggs
250 ml (1 cup) castor sugar
125 ml (½ cup) buttermilk
5 ml (1 tsp) vanilla essence
4 large ripe bananas, mashed
10 ml (2 tsp) baking powder
1 ml (¼ tsp) bicarbonate of soda
750 ml (3 cups) self-raising flour
1 Flake chocolate

Preheat the oven to 180 °C.

Beat the eggs and castor sugar till thick and creamy. Add the buttermilk and vanilla essence and mix well. Add the mashed bananas and mix well to combine. Sift in the baking powder and bicarbonate of soda. Sift in 250 ml (1 cup) of flour at a time and beat well after each addition, till a thick batter forms.

Grease a standard size loaf tin with butter and dust with flour. Spoon the batter into the tin and even out with a spatula. Sprinkle the top of the loaf with Flake and press slightly with a spoon, ensuring the chocolate seeps into the batter. Bake for 30–45 minutes. After 30 minutes, insert a skewer and if it comes out wet, bake for a few more minutes. If the skewer is dry, then remove the cake and allow to cool slightly in the tin before turning out on a wire rack to cool completely. Slice and serve warm.

VANILLA CHIFFON CAKE

MAKES 1 LARGE ROUND CAKE

THIS CAKE IS A REAL FAVOURITE AT PARTIES.

5 extra-large eggs, separated
250 ml (1 cup) castor sugar
125 ml (½ cup) cooking oil
250 ml (1 cup) boiling water, cooled slightly
5 ml (1 tsp) vanilla essence
250 ml (1 cup) cake flour
15 ml (1 Tbsp) baking powder
1 ml (¼ tsp) cream of tartar
1 x 395 g tin caramel, stirred till smooth
250 ml (1 cup) fresh cream, whipped
Sliced strawberries or chopped nuts to decorate

CHOCOLATE TOPPING
1 x 250 g slab plain milk chocolate, melted
1 x 170 g tin Nestlé dessert cream
125 ml (½ cup) fresh cream

To make the cake: Preheat the oven to 180 °C. In a large mixing bowl, cream the egg yolks and castor sugar till thick and creamy. Add the cooking oil and beat well. Next, add the boiling water and vanilla essence and mix. Sift in the flour and baking powder and beat till smooth. In a separate bowl, whisk the egg whites with the cream of tartar till soft peak stage. Using a large metal spoon, fold the stiff egg whites into the batter till well incorporated. Grease one large, deep, round cake tin (internal dimensions 29 cm x 9.5 cm deep) with butter and pour in the batter. Or use two round tins, 10 cm in diameter, and divide mixture into two. Spread evenly with a spatula and bake in the preheated oven for 30–35 minutes. Insert a long skewer into the cake and if it comes out clean, the cake is ready. Leave to cool slightly in the tin before removing. Mix all of the topping ingredients together to form a shiny chocolate glaze.

To assemble the cake: Cut the cake into three layers and sandwich the layers with caramel and whipped cream. Leave the top layer plain. Pour over the chocolate topping and decorate with strawberry slices or chopped nuts.

CAKES AND BISCUITS

This delicious cake is great to serve at tea time.

250 g butter or margarine, softened
300 ml (1 ¼ cups) castor sugar
3 large eggs
10 ml (2 tsp) vanilla essence
1 x 115 g tin granadilla pulp
750 ml (3 cups) cake flour
15 ml (1 Tbsp) baking powder
1 ml (¼ tsp) bicarbonate of soda

SERVES 10

GRANADILLA CAKE

Preheat the oven to 180 °C. Cream the butter and castor sugar well together. Add the eggs, one by one, beating well after each addition, till the mixture becomes thick and creamy. Add the vanilla essence and the granadilla pulp and mix well. Sift in the flour, baking powder and bicarbonate of soda and mix to form a smooth batter.

Grease and dust a rectangular baking tin (35 cm x 25 cm x 5 cm deep) with butter and flour. Pour in the cake batter and even out with a spatula. Bake for 35–40 minutes, or till done. Remove from the oven and allow to cool slightly in the tin. Turn out onto a large tray lined with wax paper. Flip again onto another tray so that the top part of the cake faces upwards. Allow to cool completely.

TOPPING

200 g smooth cottage cheese
250 ml (1 cup) icing sugar
1 x 115 g tin granadilla pulp
Shavings of lemon rind to decorate

Mix the cottage cheese and icing sugar together to form a smooth icing and spread a thick layer over the cake. Pour the granadilla pulp over and decorate with lemon rind shavings.

CHOCOLATE-COCONUT BISCUITS

MAKES ABOUT 30, DEPENDING ON SIZE

THESE SCRUMPTIOUS BISCUITS ARE GREAT TO SERVE WITH TEA.

250 g soft butter

375 ml (1½ cups) icing sugar

125 ml (½ cup) cooking oil

5 ml (1 tsp) vanilla essence

250 ml (1 cup) desiccated coconut

250 ml (1 cup) cornflour

60 ml (¼ cup) cocoa powder

750 ml (3 cups) cake flour

1 x 200 g slab white chocolate, melted

125 ml (½ cup) chopped nuts of choice

Preheat the oven to 180 °C. Cream the butter and icing sugar together till thick and creamy. Add the cooking oil and mix well. Add the vanilla essence and mix. Add the coconut and mix thoroughly, making sure all of the coconut is incorporated. Sift in the cornflour and cocoa powder and mix well. Lastly, add the flour, 250 ml (1 cup) at a time, mixing well after each addition, to form a semi-dry biscuit dough. Roll out the dough on a lightly floured surface to a thickness of 1 cm. Cut into desired shapes with a cookie cutter. Place the biscuits on a large baking sheet, spaced slightly apart, and bake in the preheated oven for 15–20 minutes. Remove from the oven and place on a cooling rack.

Spread the melted white chocolate over the top and sprinkle with chopped nuts.

Tip: All the biscuit dough recipes in this book can be made 2–3 days in advance and placed in the freezer. Allow to thaw completely at room temperature before using.

MELTING MOMENTS

MAKES ABOUT 24

AS THE NAME SUGGESTS, THESE BISCUITS MELT AWAY IN YOUR MOUTH. THEY MAKE A DELICIOUS ANYTIME SNACK.

250 g soft butter
250 ml (1 cup) icing sugar
60 ml (¼ cup) cooking oil
250 ml (1 cup) cornflour
625 ml (2½ cups) cake flour
1 x 200 g slab plain milk chocolate, melted

Preheat the oven to 180 °C. Cream the butter and icing sugar together till thick and creamy. Add the cooking oil and mix well. Sift in the cornflour and mix. Lastly, add the flour, 250 ml (1 cup) at a time, mixing well after each addition, to form a smooth dough.

Roll out the dough on a lightly floured surface to 1 cm thick, and cut with cookie cutters into various shapes. Place on a large baking sheet and bake in the preheated oven for 15–20 minutes. Transfer to a cooling rack and allow to cool.

Decorate by dipping one half of the biscuit into melted chocolate and leave on wax paper to harden.

BUTTER BISCUITS

MAKES 24–30

THESE ARE MY ALL-TIME FAVOURITE BISCUITS. THEY ARE RICH IN TASTE AND LIGHT IN TEXTURE.

250 g soft butter

250 ml (1 cup) castor sugar

125 ml (½ cup) cooking oil

5 ml (1 tsp) vanilla essence

625 ml (2½ cups) cake flour

Preheat the oven to 180 °C. Cream the butter and castor sugar together till thick and creamy. Add the cooking oil and mix well. Add the vanilla essence and mix. Lastly, add the cake flour, 250 ml (1 cup) at a time, mixing well after each addition to form a soft dough. Roll out the dough on a lightly floured surface to about 8 mm thick. Cut out shapes with various cookie cutters. Place the biscuits on a large baking sheet and, if you like, top each biscuit with a small piece of red glacé cherry or a sprinkling of hundreds and thousands. Press lightly with the back of a teaspoon before baking, if using the hundreds and thousands. Bake in the preheated oven for 20–25 minutes, or till lightly golden.

Variation: To prepare Half-Moon Biscuits, use the same recipe but add 125 ml (½ cup) finely chopped cashew nuts before adding the flour. Divide the dough into 20 equal portions. Roll each portion into a 5-cm-long sausage shape, curve and press the ends lightly, forming a croissant or half-moon shape. Bake in the same manner. Immediately after baking, while the biscuits are still hot, dip each biscuit into icing sugar and then place on a cooling rack to cool.

COCONUT BISCUITS

MAKES 24

THESE CRISPY BISCUITS WITH A NUTTY COCONUT TEXTURE ARE ABSOLUTELY DELICIOUS.

250 g butter, softened
300 ml (1 ¼ cups) castor sugar
250 ml (1 cup) cooking oil
5 ml (1 tsp) vanilla essence
375 ml (1 ½ cups) desiccated coconut
250 ml (1 cup) cornflour
750 ml (3 cups) cake flour

Preheat the oven to 180 °C. Cream the butter and castor sugar together till thick and creamy. Add the cooking oil and mix. Add the vanilla essence and coconut and mix well. Sift in the cornflour and mix. Lastly, sift in the cake flour, 250 ml (1 cup) at a time, mixing well after each addition to form a soft dough. Set aside for 40 minutes.

Roll out the dough on a lightly floured surface to 8 mm thick, and cut out shapes. Place the biscuits on a large baking sheet and press a small piece of red glacé cherry into the centre of each biscuit. Bake in the preheated oven for 20–25 minutes. Cool on a cooling rack and store in an airtight container.

Tip: Before rolling out the dough, place it in the refrigerator for 2–3 minutes to prevent the dough from becoming too soft. This will make the dough easy to handle.

CAKES AND BISCUITS

These crunchies were a real winner among my friends at school. My mother would often bake large batches, which I would take along to school to treat my mates.

250 g soft butter
250 ml (1 cup) sugar
30 ml (2 Tbsp) golden syrup
500 ml (2 cups) rolled oats
250 ml (1 cup) chocolate chips
250 ml (1 cup) brown bread flour
250 ml (1 cup) desiccated coconut
A pinch of salt
2.5 ml (½ tsp) bicarbonate of soda
60 ml (¼ cup) full-cream milk
5 ml (1 tsp) vanilla essence

MAKES 40

CHOCOLATE CHIP CRUNCHIES

Preheat the oven to 180 °C.

Cream the butter, sugar and syrup till thick and creamy. Add the remaining ingredients and mix well. Place tablespoonsful of the mixture onto a large baking sheet and flatten slightly with the back of a spoon – leave enough space between biscuits for spreading.

Bake in the preheated oven for 15 minutes, or till golden. Transfer to a rack and allow to cool.

RECIPE INDEX

Page numbers in **bold** type indicate photographs.

BISCUITS
butter **156**, 156
chocolate chip crunchies **158**, 159
chocolate-coconut **154**, 154
coconut **157**, 157
melting moments 155, **155**

BREADS
focaccia **124**, 125
kitke rolls **122**, 123
naan bread rolls **118**, 118
puri 119, **119**
roti **120**, 121

BREYANIS
maffrou 79, **79**
mutton akhni **80**, 81
mutton breyani **84**, 85
seafood akhni **82**, 83

CAKES AND SWEET TREATS
banana loaf cake **150**, 150
chocolate swiss roll 147
éclairs **144**, 145
granadilla cake **152**, 153
never-fail chocolate cake **148**, 149
vanilla chiffon cake 151, **151**
vanilla swiss roll **146**, 147

CHICKEN DISHES
butter chicken **44**, 44
chicken pie **48**, 49
chicken tikka **46**, 46
chicken vegetable soup **12**, 13
creamy chicken and corn soup **14**, 14
crumbed chicken 41, **41**
Eid oven-roasted chicken 47, **47**
haleem **20**, 21
kalya chicken curry **72**, 73
masala tandoori chicken **42**, 43
pepper chicken pot roast **40**, 40
pumpkin curry **76**, 77
samoosas 25, **25**
sweet-and-sour chicken 45, **45**
tomato and mushroom chicken stew 93, **93**

CHOPS
braised with tomato and onion **60**, 60
denning **53**, 53
sosatie **52**, 52

CURRIES
crayfish tail **74**, 75
fish **68**, 69
kalya chicken **72**, 73
mutton **70**, 71
mutton dahl **78**, 78
pumpkin **76**, 77

FILLINGS (SAVOURY)
cheese 24
chicken 25, **25**, 49
mince 23, **23**
vegetable 24

FILLINGS (SWEET)
apple 139
chocolate 145
coconut 137
milk tart 136
strawberry cream 145

FISH AND SEAFOOD DISHES
baked snoek **30**, 31
Cape grilled crayfish **36**, 36
crayfish tail curry **74**, 75
fish cakes **32**, 32
fish curry **68**, 69
fish frikkadels **28**, 28
garlic grilled prawns **34**, 35
green masala kingklip 33, **33**
pickled fish 37, **37**
salmon smoor **29**, 29
seafood akhni **82**, 83

FRITTERS
banana 141
potato **140**, 140
pumpkin 141, **141**

MEAT DISHES
bobotie **58**, 59
braised chops with tomato and onion **60**, 60
braised steak **56**, 57
cabbage bredie 89, **89**
carrots and peas stew **92**, 92
creamy pepper steak 65, **65**
denning chops 53, **53**

haleem **20**, 21
maffrou 79, **79**
masala steak 61, **61**
mince kebabs **62**, 63
mutton akhni **80**, 81
mutton breyani **84**, 85
mutton curry **70**, 71
mutton dahl curry **78**, 78
pot roast leg of lamb **54**, 55
pumpkin bredie **88**, 88
samoosas 23, **23**
sosatie chops **52**, 52
split pea soup 15, **15**
traditional corned beef **64**, 64

PIES
chicken **48**, 49

PUDDINGS
bread pudding **134**, 134
lockshen delight 133
potato pudding with stewed fruit **128**, 129
sago pudding 135, **135**
trifle **130**, 131
vermicelli (lockshen) **132**, 133

RICE
braised white **97**, 97
flop-proof white 101, **101**
kitchri **100**, 100
savoury **98**, 99
sweet yellow **96**, 96

ROASTS
Eid oven-roasted chicken 47, **47**
pepper chicken pot roast **40**, 40
pot roast leg of lamb **54**, 55

SALADS
baked bean 111, **111**
egg 115, **115**
tomato and onion **112**, 113
tuna **114**, 114

SAUCES
creamy garlic 35
tomato gravy 91
tzatziki 57

SNACKS
dhaltjies (chilli bites) **16**, 17
potato bites **18**, 19
potato fritters **140**, 140
pumpkin fritters 141, **141**
salmon smoor **29**, 29
samoosas 22–25, **23**, **25**

SOUPS
chicken vegetable **12**, 13
creamy chicken and corn **14**, 14
haleem **20**, 21
split pea 15, **15**

STEAKS
braised **56**, 57
creamy pepper 65, **65**
masala 61, **61**

STEWS AND BREDIES
cabbage bredie 89, **89**
carrots and peas stew **92**, 92
pumpkin bredie **88**, 88
tomato and mushroom chicken stew 93, **93**
tomato frikkadel bredie **90**, 91

TARTS
apple crumble **138**, 139
coconut tartlets 137, **137**
milk tart **136**, 136

TOPPINGS
chocolate 149, 151
granadilla 153

VEGETABLE AND VEGETARIAN DISHES
cauliflower and broccoli bake **108**, 108
cinnamon sweet pumpkin **104**, 105
glazed carrots **106**, 106
green bean bajie 107, **107**
peri-peri potato wedges **110**, 110
potato bites **18**, 19
potato fritters **140**, 140
pumpkin fritters 141, **141**
samoosas 24
stewed sweet potato 109, **109**